Woman Alone

A Six-Month Journey Through the Australian Outback

LAINE CUNNINGHAM

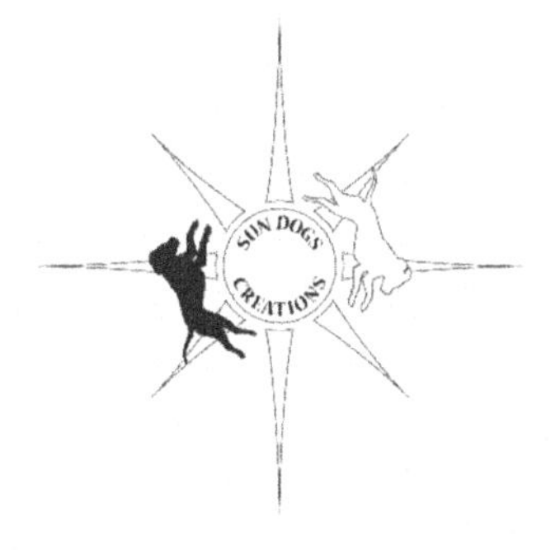

Woman Alone

A Six-Month Journey Through the Australian Outback

Published by Sun Dogs Creations
Changing the World One Book at a Time

Cover Design by Angel Leya

ISBN: 9780998224022

Praise for Laine Cunningham's Books

"Laine Cunningham combines tenacity and courage along with profound insight. Her bravery is contagious. I keep Laine's books on a special shelf in my library, referring to them when I need inspiration."

—Pamela King Cable, Author, *The Sanctum* and *Televenge*

"The fact that Laine Cunningham spent six long months on her own in the Australian outback before writing this book leant a rich authenticity to her voice as she shared from her abundantly full, and talented, heart."

—Leah Griffith, Author, *Cosette's Tribe*

"Demonstrates a mastery of psychological introspection and an uncanny feel for the spirit of place."

—James Jones Literary Society

"Mesmerizing and meaningful an inspiring."

—Grady Harp, Vine Voice

"An exceptional writer as well as a master storyteller."

—Edmund R. Shubert, Author and Editor for Tor

"An affirmation of life."

—Shirley, Goodreads Reviewer

"I thought this book would be a quick read, but I found myself lingering, absorbing the message ... I found this book to be both entertaining and informative, one I will probably reread quite a few times."

—Dena Harris, Author

Table of Contents

Introduction

SOME YEARS AGO, I did something that most people, depending on their taste for risk, might consider daring, adventurous, or idiotic. I chucked everything to spend six months camping—alone, as a woman—in the Australian Outback.

Sounds bold, maybe, unless you know that the life I had constructed stick by stick and day by day was empty. The college degree that suited my goals as a novelist left me unsuited to a wide range of income-producing options, so I had landed in a corporate job I utterly despised.

My depression wasn't clinical—I functioned well enough and held down a job and ate regularly and exercised—but I was anything except happy. Every morning I dragged myself into an office building where my peers viciously tore down the overweight woman on our team, invented horribly clever and horribly misogynistic nicknames for our boss (most of my peers were women), and gossiped endlessly about who was sleeping with whom and what that might mean for the woman's career advancement (never the man's).

I lived in a basement apartment with so many health and safety violations that the police officer who arrived when my car was broken into offered to report my landlord. I declined because I would have been forced to find another place I could afford, a tall order in the Washington, DC metropolitan area.

I had tons of friends and went out nearly every weekend but the bar scene and the punk rock scene and the all-night party/hookup scene and the hanging out at movie night getting stoned scene had grown stale even before I'd received my degree. I had already dedicated myself to becoming a writer but was too mentally exhausted to get much writing done.

And that was the real problem. Because I wasn't pursuing my true place in the world, the life I was leading—corporatized, industrialized, and in which everything I had ever been taught to want had been falsely glamorized—was killing me.

Something had to be done. What, I wasn't exactly sure. For a year, I reached out to my company's London office. My father's family is at least half Scotts-Irish, so the transfer would have opened up explorations into that side of my heritage.

By the time the foreign office's director made it clear—through a blunt, face-to-face conversation that materialized only because we both happened to arrive at the deserted Virginia office at six in the morning—that an offer would never be extended, my backup plan had already been funded with a fat savings account.

The idea was to knock around in the UK until the money ran out. I hoped to be there for a year but the expenses made it much more likely I would only wander for six months. I would see the sights, visit the rolling countryside, and work on losing as much of my tan as any self-respecting UK citizen. Who knew what might arise during that time? Where might I land?

I applied for a sabbatical and started packing. Anything I wouldn't truly need when...if...I returned to the US was sold off or given away. The rest was stored in my parents' basement. Even the car I had so lovingly restored, and into which I had sunk a feverish amount of money, was put up for sale. The Triumph was too temperamental to sit unattended for six hours let alone six months, so selling it was the best option.

As the final sixty days ticked away, something bizarre and unsettling happened. Time and again, I was visited by vivid dreams of kangaroos and the red desert. Over the course of a few weeks, the images went from foggy to sharply intense.

These dream-visions never came when I was deeply asleep. Instead they appeared like beautiful hallucinations whenever I was drowsing. Their gravitational pull caught at my heart. As I rose up out of each one, its threads and its images clung to me for minutes and then hours.

Finally I surrendered. All right, already! I'll go to Australia!

I knew nothing about the country or what I might do there. But one thing was clear: this journey I had decided to take had always been about the Outback...even before I'd started dreaming.

That was perfectly fine with me. I'd considered hiking through America's largest national parks for a year but I really wanted to leave the country. Rather than walk the UK's cliffs and moors, perhaps I could camp in the desert.

No matter how I spent my time in Australia, though, something was waiting for me. Something had grown tired of waiting and was reaching out. I bought the ticket.

The frenzied preparations that went with switching destinations began. My division head had already said the company would not guarantee that my position would be open when I returned. In my mind, there was no guarantee that I would return to that company or even to the US.

With less than two weeks to go, I took a nap on the couch. As I drifted closer toward sleep, I fell into a vision of astonishing clarity. My spirit soared over red desert plains where a few stunted trees dotted the broad earth. I swooped down toward a lone tree with a twisted black trunk. Its thin canopy cast jagged shadows over a corpse.

My corpse. I floated inches above it, peering at the face to be certain that it was me and that I was dead. A film of dust coated eyes that stared blankly at the sky.

The shock jolted me awake. I sat for a long time thinking about how clear and detailed the vision had been. Was this a warning? I was twenty-seven years old. Any trip a woman undertakes alone involves risks, and wandering through undeveloped regions in a foreign country would entail dangers of which I was ignorant. This wasn't supposed to be a suicide mission. Should I cancel the trip?

In a way, though, I was already dead. Returning to the life I had been living was unthinkable. The depression that weighed me down, the sheer grind of sameness at my job, the poisonous gossip and the stretch of similar days would never end unless something was done...done by me, and done for me.

I decided to go. Even if I died in the outback, for a few short months—and really for the first time in my life—I would have lived fully.

I told no one about the vision. Too many opinions had already been proffered about my plans. My parents were of course worried but knew it was hopeless to try to dissuade me. My friends thought it was great while pointing out the homes, children, and responsibilities that prevented them from undertaking the same type of journey. My department head didn't think I'd last more than two months before begging for my job back. Who would I tell?

Halfway through the journey, I would find that lonely, twisted tree. The events that would take place there would threaten my life and be entirely out of my control...until, that is, I made a choice.

A choice made by me. A choice made for me.

That experience and my choice would change me forever. After finding that tree, the rest of my time in the Outback would be different. It would feel less compelling, as if marking that milepost had accomplished everything I'd come to achieve.

Eventually I realized that it had marked the turning point I'd hoped to find. My life before that tree had been so flawed that the escape hatch had been hidden. Still I'd known, or my heart had known, that a new road would lead to more than just surviving in a salaried position, more than just getting through every day by keeping my head down and my mouth shut.

Only a dramatic and dangerous event could reveal that road. Only facing death allowed me to choose life.

Before I headed into the Outback, the many people who had confessed that they wanted to do something similar also said that their kids, their spouse, their mortgage, their whatever were insurmountable obstacles that prevented them from undertaking their own journeys.

The truth is that they were also making a choice. They were bypassing one dream in order to pursue or maintain a different dream they valued more. Before my sabbatical, I purged nearly all my material possessions. That left the entire world open to possibility...even the possibility that my life would end.

Not everyone can or should take such drastic steps. But people who allow other considerations to overshadow their dreams should let go of the vision or idea or concept that actually isn't their dream. Stability, raising a family, and cultivating a life that's filled with comfort and joy are all dreams that can be fulfilled...if the dreamers are willing to make conscious and informed choices.

No matter what your dream looks like, my wish is that the book you're holding right now provides the hope and inspiration to launch you onto your own path. In these pages, you'll find the usual traveler's stories brightly painted with the ways other people live. You'll read some of my comments and hear the thoughts of others. Along the way, perhaps you'll find an undiscovered part of yourself. Perhaps you'll mark your own milestone.

Turn the page with every hope for the person you can become.

Touchdown, Sydney

AUSTRALIA IS THE SOLO TRAVELER'S PARADISE. During my journey, the government had set aside public parking lots where private owners could sell their cars. Dealers were not allowed to sell there, so the vehicles were passed from one sojourner to another. The practice continues today; travelers will also find that a number of used-car lots will sell them a car with the promise to buy back their vehicle for roughly 50% of what was paid.

After a week of searching and considering whether to buy a four-wheel-drive vehicle—which would require quite a bit of maintenance—or a standard car, I settled on a twenty-year-old Ford Falcon sedan. The four doors would make loading and unloading the camping gear easier. The motor was an eight-cylinder, a much better choice than the four-cylinder vehicles that would struggle to survive the heat, the dust, and the long distances.

I was inordinately pleased with the metal mule. Americans have a long-standing love affair with cars and the open road, and the ability to travel freely would be an important part of my journey.

My ecstasy was a bit dampened by the terrifying realities of sitting behind the wheel. Although I had studied Australian traffic rules, getting used to the signs while negotiating city traffic was nerve-wracking.

The right-hand drive didn't help. For the longest time I had to remind myself to drive on the left, and learning how to execute a smooth right turn without smacking a pedestrian made me sweat.

Fortunately the car's former owner had plastered a Danish Kingdom sticker on the rear window. My foreign status was boldly advertised, so other drivers refrained from honking too often.

The gas tank was nearly empty when I was handed the keys, so the first task was to fill up. Creeping into the nearest station, I parked in front of a pump that had been padlocked with a chain. The attendant barely looked up when I walked in and asked for help with the gas.

"Sorry, we haven't any gas," he said.

"You've run out?" I asked.

"No, we don't sell that here."

"You don't sell *gas* here?"

A light flickered behind his eyes. "You'll be wanting *auto*gas, yes?"

"Yes," I breathed, relieved that the language barrier had crumbled. "I want gas for the auto."

"We don't sell that here."

I was flummoxed. A filling station open for business but with nothing to sell? The profit margin on those candy bars must have been pretty high. Feeling unbelievably stupid, I asked, "This is a gas station?"

"Oh!" He snapped the magazine shut. "You'll be wanting *petrol* for your auto."

And so the adventure began.

Orphan

THE FIRST WEEK OR SO was spent ambling along the highway heading west from Sydney. A long pause in the Blue Mountains allowed me to become acquainted with the camping lifestyle without missing out on showers or flush toilets. Atop that ridge, I awoke every morning to the complex warbling of the Australian magpie. This birthed an obsession with birds that brings me joy to this day.

While on the Blue Mountains, I also lost my watch. Cell phones still weren't affordable or even very portable at the time, so losing the watch cut me off from any concept of time other than the movement of the sun, the arc of the moon, and the hunger that visited regularly throughout the day. The loss was a blessing that created a fundamental shift in my lifestyle.

Eventually I moved along to Adelaide, South Australia. The city welcomed me on a Sunday bustling with tourists and casual drivers. A woman I had made contact with earlier welcomed me into her home for a short time.

Mary was in her sixties with a full head of gray hair curled into fluffy waves. She never wore pants and was always smartly outfitted in a skirt and blouse. In some ways she was the definition of matronly, especially when she twittered with relief at my safe arrival.

"I'm so glad you're all right," she said. "I've been so worried!"

She fanned the air as if to dispel any harmful spirits. Then she ushered me into her house, a single-story cottage tucked behind a pretty front yard rimmed with an unpainted picket fence.

The house was surprisingly narrow, and the long hallway led past several bedrooms before opening up into the kitchen where she and her husband spent most of their time. Mary and Michael were originally from the United Kingdom. They had lived in Australia half their lives before retiring.

I had worked with one of Mary's distant relatives and, a week before leaving, had called for travel advice. Despite my long list of questions about camping equipment, the cost of different things, and the desert, the conversation lasted only a few minutes.

"You just forget about all that," she said. "I have an extra room where you can stay, and I'll take care of everything. When will you be here?"

By the third call, the guest room had been repainted and Mary had rung my mother to assure her I would be safe. When I showed up, she insisted I call my parents before guiding me to my room.

The space was as large as any of the other rooms with fourteen-foot ceilings and gauzy curtains shielding two tall windows. She had cleared space in the dresser and left for a few minutes so I could unpack.

While I put my things away, Mary went down the street to pick up some food for our first meal. She returned with a load that rivaled the crab feast my family used to set up for our annual reunion. After the plate had been filled from rim to rim, she piled food on top and occasionally spooned up more as I ate.

She seemed determined to feed me until I fell over. I quickly learned to keep my elbows firmly planted on the table to shield the dish from her unlimited benevolence. I had roamed thousands of miles to stay with someone who out-mothered my own mother.

Mary regularly took in people she called "orphans," students and backpackers who otherwise would have been relegated to the communal rooms of hostels. Almost every foray to the shops was an opportunity to discover another stray.

Once she returned from the grocers all aflutter because she had offered her house to a Catholic girls' choir whose hotel reservations had fallen through. She wasn't sure she had enough floor space but, as always, everyone received lodgings.

The Way to a Galah's Heart

MARY AND MICHAEL'S LONG COTTAGE, including the guest room, was ruled by a rose-breasted cockatoo. Aussies called the birds galahs, a term derived from the Yuwaalaraay and neighboring Aboriginal tribes who called them *gilaa.* When released from his cage, Bobby paraded in military strides over to my feet and then crawled up my pant leg to say hello.

I didn't realize that he would do this repeatedly. The next morning during breakfast, he marched under the table and clambered up my pants. When I stood up, I accidentally launched him across the linoleum.

He shrieked endlessly at me as Mary clucked and cooed. I loved animals of all types, so I felt terrible about this poor start to our relationship. And, of course, this first of what would be many run-ins with the native animals did not bode well for the rest of my journey.

In an attempt to repair my budding friendship with Bobby, I groveled every evening before his perch with mashed potatoes from my plate. Those humble moments taught me exactly how unforgiving a cockatoo could be.

He ignored my tithe even as he demanded the same food from his mistress. With the first rattle of skillets in the afternoon, he and Mary began a habitual dance.

"Mary," he sang pleasantly.

"What?" she sang back with a misty smile. "My little Bobby. He knows I'm cooking."

She abandoned the pots to boil and the pans to bake, and padded over to his cage. Holding her arms wide, she leaned near the bars.

"Come give mommy a kiss," she said.

Bobby spread his wings and shoved his beak through the bars. She delivered a kiss as his tongue wriggled. Then she returned to the stove.

"Mary," he warbled.

Preoccupied by food and steam and smells, she did not hear—or perhaps she ignored—his calls. Soon his tone became ardent.

"Mary!" he snapped.

"What, Bobby?" she demanded as her own patience wore thin.

"Mary!" he yelled. "Mar-*rink! Rink-rink-rink!"*

His calls were tinny and angry. He dangled from the top of the cage flipping his pink crest and flapping his wings. When she waved her finger at the bars, Bobby nipped the air.

"Stop that!" she said. "No bities. No bities!"

When he was finally subdued, she padded back to the stove. Through the silence and steam, the bird attempted to make amends.

"I love you," he mumbled.

"You only love me because you want dinner."

"Mar-rink! Rink-rink!"

"Oh, all right!" She dished up a spoonful of mashed potatoes. "Here, you fool bird, now be quiet. Hot, Bobby, hot!"

Michael also waged a low-level war with Bobby, although with considerably more ire. He didn't like the bird, perhaps in part because the galah was insanely jealous of Mary's affection. Although Bobby was a mere seven inches tall, he attacked Michael at every opportunity.

With his wings clipped, he couldn't fly at him and instead nipped his ankles and gnawed his shoes. Whenever Michael sat in his favorite spot, an overstuffed armchair near the cage, Bobby switched to a verbal assault.

"Move it!" he shrilled. "Move it!"

Michael simply shut off his hearing aid. While he might have enjoyed his evening paper in the living room, whenever he settled next to that cage, a tiny smile of satisfaction played across his lips.

Road Robbers

SUPPER, ALSO CALLED TEA, was served early the day of my departure so that Mary could watch me eat one last hearty meal. Even though she had arranged for me to stay with her daughter in Coober Pedy, she fretted and fussed while packing sandwiches and juice. Eventually she joined Michael, Bobby and I at the table where she rubbed her face and peered through the smoke of her cigarette.

"Now, you know not to stop for anyone, don't you?" she asked. "And you particularly don't stop for those black fellows, those Aborigines. They'll make you think they need help and steal your petrol. Bugger you! Leave you there!"

Race relations in Australia were not optimal. As had happened in America, European immigrants had flowed in for two hundred years and set up an entirely different way of life. Over time, laws had been enacted that displaced the tribes. The government moved them to restricted areas like Native American reservations; it also implemented immigration laws that favored white Europeans over other nationalities.

Eventually the places where Aboriginal people lived evolved into land claims. Those regions had been ceded back to the original tribes and were run much like the sovereign lands of Native American peoples. There the indigenous people were able to live according to their own laws and traditions.

The situation created strife on both sides. Families who had ranched or lived on a parcel of land for several generations feared the loss of everything their grandparents and parents had built if a claim was filed against their property. The tribal people, meanwhile, were able to claw back only small portions of what once had been theirs...or, in accordance with their beliefs, land that had belonged to no one except the spirits that lived in those areas.

Wherever there is fear, racism arises. Although I had only been in the country for about a month, I had already been told many fables: Aborigines would pretend to need assistance and flag down vehicles only to steal the petrol. A single black man or woman would stand by the road hitchhiking; when someone stopped to pick them up, eight friends who had been hiding in the bush would step out and expect a ride.

Although I knew the stories were bull, I didn't know what to make of the quickness with which they were offered. I never had to ask about dangers or even mention Aboriginal peoples before the tales were dragged out. My awareness of racism in America came from having lived in a dozen states before attending college. What I found in Australia was a new level altogether.

Mary really seemed to believe the stories. While she talked, she grew more and more upset imagining a woman alone in the Outback. She chaffed and churned, patting her neck and tugging her hair, desperate to offer some type of assistance. Then she rushed to a cabinet to rummage through a jumble of miscellaneous treasures.

"Here, you take this," she said. "Oh dear, where is it, now? It's here, don't leave yet. Ah!"

She forced a shiny object into my hands.

"If any of those black fellows try to pull you over," she said, "wave this at them and they'll be scared and run away."

She had given me a toy cap gun.

Woman Alone

THE TRIP FROM Sydney to Adelaide had crossed New South Wales, one of Australia's six large states. New South Wales was the country's most populated area, and my path had run from the narrow coastal strip across the western slopes and plains to Adelaide's subtropical region. The journey had been filled with forests that to my eyes looked spare and thin.

When I left Mary and Michael's home, I headed north. Finally I would enter the vast red desert that dominated much of Australia's land mass. It was the essence of the dreams that had driven me to change directions, and I was impatient to begin what I felt was the important part of my trip.

The Outback did not disappoint. The flat plains wore the extravagance of distance and simplicity. What little scrub did manage to grow crouched low beneath the sun. Groups of twisted eucalyptus trees, called mallee, were cloaked in tapered leaves that flashed whip-edged in the wind.

Although few people lived on this land, the signs of their passing were everywhere. Litter overflowed the occasional trash bins staked beside the road as if the verdant parks they had served had disappeared.

Abandoned vehicles stripped of glass and rubber and chrome hunkered behind bushes. The remains were rusted, sun-bleached, and somehow haunted. One had flipped onto its roof, clearly an accident; others sprawled on their hubs like murder victims.

Because the distance I needed to cross was encompassed by a government-owned restricted area with only one public road, the number of travelers was relatively high. The first night, I stopped at a roadhouse intending to pitch my tent nearby. The rough-looking men who hung around in the parking lot drinking had little to do except watch me. I slept in the car with the doors locked.

Opal Fever

THE NEXT MORNING, I was up early and headed out again. Long hours passed until the hypnotic landscape changed. Then Coober Pedy, an opal mining town, sprouted in lumps that marred the horizon. As I drew closer, the mounds grew as if an army of mutant ants had been very busy. Each was a pile of chalky dirt that chronicled an abandoned claim.

The town itself was tiny, a few thousand souls squeezed into a small patch in the middle of the fields. Everything about the place exuded the final asthmatic wheeze of a bust farm community. The buildings and cars were coated with a patina of red grit that made even the newest construction look vaguely ramshackle, much as California's towns must have appeared during the gold rush.

Dust puffed across the road like smoky jellyfish. Everything was hard: the packed earthen shoulders, the sun-bleached asphalt road, the walls of the cinderblock and concrete shops. Nothing except a few scraggly vegetable gardens grew within town limits. Water was far too precious to waste on flowers and trees and grass.

Mary had introduced me to her daughter Marie and her son-in-law David when they stopped in for a visit. They had provided a few tips for driving on the Outback roads before sketching a mud map to their home. While doing so, they had cursed the recent naming of their street because it meant things were being developed. They grumpily conceded that the town might soon have a traffic light.

Their idea of urban blight, however, did not include the paving of the road. Bulldust, the red talcum powder that swirled atop the desert plains, became a pasty muck in the rain. During the dry season, the dirt tracks shook loose a vehicle's every screw and bolt. Even machines spared the rough opal fields fell to ruin from the insidious dust.

Everything about Coober Pedy was rough and ready. The mail arrived a few times a week in a small, two-engine plane, fresh groceries were delivered only once a week, and mining operations were performed mostly by individuals or small groups who pooled their resources.

David and Marie shared a claim with two other individuals. Between them, they had enough equipment, money, and manpower to make a living. David carted me along one day to show me how they worked.

The opal field was a barren place pocked with holes. Beside every shaft rose a white hill made of slag, the dirt that had been moved to uncover the opal veins. Because there were so many open shafts, David instructed me to turn fully around and look at the ground even when walking only a few feet. There were too many chances to drop down a hole.

He was on the mine rescue squad, a group of volunteers who were experienced enough with mining to pull victims—or their bodies—out of the shafts. He spent much of his time saving shutterbugs who had backed up while framing that perfect picture and taken one step too far.

The ease with which anyone could get into trouble was so extreme that tour groups were no longer allowed off the buses. Even so, individual tourists often drove or walked out into the fields. The squad had already pulled three visitors out of the ground that year. As David told me their stories, he fixed me with a bug-eyed stare.

"Every bloody one of them was an American," he said, "and a woman."

David's humor was only half joking. A number of Aussies I met along the way—plenty of whom were female—held fairly regressive ideas about women. One of those ideas was that women were not terribly capable of taking care of themselves.

Then again, anyone who spent their time pulling the careless and the foolish out of mine shafts wasn't going to harbor a strong faith in humanity.

"One of the women we hauled out was soaked in blood," he said. "All the blood come from just a little cut. Another young lady bawled nonstop for her mama, so we figured she'd be fine. We got her up and on her feet, and a minute later she collapsed. The fall burst a vein near her spinal column. She bled to death internally."

Experience in the fields didn't guarantee safety. The work was demanding even for the most skilled, and during my stay a miner met with tragedy. He was working alone with a rock driller outfitted with a huge auger. When shiny pieces appeared on the outside of the bit, the machine was removed and mining continued by hand.

As this miner watched, a large chunk of opal flashed in the bit. The stone, which was large enough to promise an exceptional payday, would be crushed inside the auger. When he snatched at the gem, the bit caught his sleeve. His forearm was pulled into the auger and twisted off. The torque also shattered the bones in his upper arm.

After applying a tourniquet, he tucked the severed limb beneath what remained of his ruined arm. Then he hopped into his sling, rode the winch slowly to the surface, and stumbled to the only other mine being worked that day. The local clinic, the sole provider of medical help for hundreds of miles, could do little more than pack the arm in ice and prevent further blood loss.

The Royal Flying Doctor, an emergency airlift that provided ambulance service in the country's vast interior, arrived within an unexpectedly short two hours. The Royal Adelaide Hospital reattached the limb and within seventy-two hours, blood flow had been miraculously reestablished.

No one doubted that the miner would return to Coober Pedy as soon as he was able to work his claim.

Crystal Fire

DURING MY DAY IN THE OPAL FIELDS, I stuck close as David explained the business of prospecting. First, a drill rig punched through the earth like a spiny echidna crunching through a termite mound. The soil that was pulled up was examined for opal and potch, the girasol that made up most of a vein.

Opal is formed from silica. Large deposits were laid down in Australia millennium ago. Five to six million years later, opal measuring about 1 centimeter had matured. The gem doesn't have a crystalline structure like rubies, so the silica refracts light into various colors.

Since so much time was needed for opal to mature, the immature sediment, called girasol or potch, often indicated that opal could be found. When girasol appeared in the dirt excavated from the exploratory hole, a larger shaft was bored as the entry point. The original tunnel became an exit point for slag.

David's claim was an unmarked, gaping hole. It looked to me like all the other shafts but this one was active. A pole laid across the opening supported a steel ladder. An electrical cord and a few ropes snaked into the burrow; electricity was needed for the lights and mining equipment while the ropes were used to send equipment up and down.

The ground around the hole sloped toward the dark maw and made the footing unsure. David said I could still back out. When the loose shale shifted beneath my boots, my breath caught in my heart. My healthy respect for heights kicked in, because what was that seventy-foot shaft other than a seventy-foot fall? As crazy as ever, I said I still wanted to join them.

Before we descended, a few tasks had to be completed. We hovered over the truck bed and assembled explosive charges from a few sheets of newsprint, fertilizer, a length of fuse and masking tape. The only challenging part of the homemade approach was to tamp the nitrate down properly.

"I should have an explosives sign on the truck," David said. "If you go to the drive-in theater, there's a sign at the entrance that reads *No Explosives.* Bloody idiots drink too much and smoke in their cars. That makes for too many accidents."

The detonating caps, which would be gently crimped onto the fuses, were left to one of the other team members named Mark.

"Last year," David mused, "a fellah lit up a cig and a hot ash fell in the box of caps. Only the caps blew but there wasn't anything left to retrieve. No real pieces, you know. We just sort of wiped him up."

Mark warmed up the blower, which was basically a giant vacuum bolted onto a flatbed truck. The pipe that led from the equipment down into the mine would suck out the dross and dump it a short distance from the entrance. It would also remove the poisonous fumes after the explosives had been detonated.

Mark went down first, and I watched carefully as he crouched near the hole and gently pitched forward. After catching himself on the crossbeam, he swung his feet onto the ladder. I copied him exactly as David held onto the back of my jacket in case I slipped.

"Never, ever look up the shaft," he warned. "If you do, you'll likely get a smack from a rock. Edward did it all the time until one day I chucked a wrench down the hole. He caught the wrench with his mouth."

Then he released my jacket. I was on my own.

Seventy Feet Under

THE COLD RUNGS ROSE MONOTONOUSLY as I felt for each foothold. A constant rain of dust and rock pinged off the hard hat. I heard only the oddly metallic echo of my movements and my own excited breath.

A tumble probably would not have been fatal, David had said. People bumped into the sides of the shafts as they went down, which broke their fall. I was careful nevertheless. My toe finally scraped earth, and I hunched over to peer into the underworld.

A storage nook to the left shielded the equipment during blasting. Other than common sense and the team's experience, safety features were glaringly absent. The walls and ceilings of the tunnel weren't braced against cave-ins, and the only supply of fresh air was sucked in by the blower as it shifted dirt out of the mine. During rains—or afterward as runoff sluiced across the flat terrain—mines could suddenly flood.

The work occurred further along the tunnel created as the vein was chased. Progress was slow. Using pickaxes and a handheld jackhammer, the men dug out above and below the girasol. As each tired, they relinquishing the equipment to the next worker.

Whenever the shift changed, they chided each other with genial insults. Taking up the tools again brought complete silence as they watched the dirt fall away. The tiniest glimmer signaled mature opal, the green and red fire that would pad their bank accounts long enough to continue mining or make them all rich.

"Come on," David mumbled. "Where is it? Where's the bloody opal?"

When the vein shimmied deeper into the wall, the pickaxes and jackhammer were no longer useful. Mark drilled five deep cavities that would each receive one explosive. I climbed back up to safety with the other two men as he tinkered with the detonating caps. If he had an accident, only one person would be injured.

Eventually he joined us. Each stick of dynamite would go off a few seconds after the other, allowing the team to count the blasts. If one of the explosives failed to detonate, someone—again only a single person to reduce the number of injuries or deaths—would have to go down and fix things.

“No matter how many years I mine,” David said, “the first explosion always makes me jump.”

The wind swirled the dust. With the first muffled bang, the ground trembled like a horse twitching at flies. The rest followed at relatively equal intervals. We counted one through five and relaxed only after the final explosion.

Frontier Justice

WHILE THE BLOWER removed the poisonous fumes, we munched sandwiches and snacks. Perhaps drawn by the explosions, a fellow with a face wrinkled from years of squinting into the glare doddered over. Accompanying him were half a dozen motley dogs. The pack snuffled at us and the ground, friendly but alert to any scraps we might have dropped.

The man lived in a trailer parked on an abandoned claim. Since he owned the trailer, he needed only enough money to buy food and clothes...although judging by what he wore that day, he didn't often bother to replace what he had. He eked out a living by noodling, the slang term for sifting through the slag for opal.

The miners knew that chunks could end up in the refuse mounds as easily as their pockets. A number of them noodled their slag with large mesh screens like the ones used in archaeological digs. Others couldn't be bothered, so anyone could hunt for treasure the minute the slag hit the ground.

David offered the man a few packets of tobacco and a stack of rolling papers. In return, he would keep an eye on the claim. The steel ladder was lowered in ten-foot increments into the hole, and because of its weight, was left in place. During the night, poachers could slip down and, for the cost of a pickax and a few hours, walk away with the owner's opal.

Even people with their own mines might become poachers. Although most workers usually abandoned the vein when they drew close to the border, avarice...or a bout of opal fever...could pursued them to dig far past the edges of their mine and into someone else's.

People who were caught poaching could be fined AU$1,000 per foot. But that assumed that the criminal would be caught. If no one bought the adjoining claim or if the adjoining claim didn't dig far enough to discover the theft, it was an easy crime. Even after discovery, a dishonest bloke could always say that someone else must have dug past the border after the mine had been abandoned.

The realities of how the law worked in towns as isolated as Coober Pedy meant that unofficial punishments were occasionally dealt. Earlier that month a blower, which cost about AU$50,000, had caught on fire. At night. For no apparent mechanical reason.

Everyone knew the real reason, though. The owner of the equipment had allegedly been caught poaching a few months before. He'd used the usual excuses to evade the official law. Frontier justice, however, was not so easily avoided.

Death in the Fields

"HOW DO YOU LIKE MINING, THEN?" Marie asked over dinner. "Dirty work, hey?"

"Yeah," I said. "It reminds me of a temporary job I had as a maintenance worker. At the end of the day I could point to all the things I had finished. It was really satisfying. That kind of job will last a lifetime."

"I don't know about mining lasting a lifetime," she said. "But it's a living."

The nightly soaps distracted us for a time, and we ate until the sharp edge of hunger had been dulled. During a commercial, I fished for information about the dashing single fellow on the mining team.

"Mark offered to buy me a drink if I'm still around Friday night," I said.

Marie snapped to attention. "No matter who it is or what anyone offers," she said, "you don't go anywhere in this town without one of the family."

Her eyes did not flicker as she said, "There's a killer in Coober Pedy."

"What?"

"He's taken two women already," she said. "At first, when the traveler disappeared, they thought a transient offered her a ride and away they went."

When I'd first arrived in Australia, I had been surprised by the number of people who hitchhiked. People often left their hometowns to find seasonal employment or for vacations. International visitors did the same, and every hostel and roadhouse had a message board where people could ask for or offer rides.

A number of those individuals went missing every year. Not all of them were women, either. Unless a body was found, officials assumed that the person didn't want to be found—a likely occurrence given the ease with which someone could disappear by moving to a remote town—or that they had died by getting lost, getting stuck without food or water, or succumbing to other desert dangers.

Despite those events, a vast number of people still hitchhiked. It had been safe enough for long enough that asking for a ride from a complete stranger was common. But even in Australia, things were changing.

"The second woman to go missing," Marie said, "was a young Aborigine, a pretty little thing. Everyone knew she was too smart to get into a car with anyone she didn't know. So whoever took her is from our community."

"They haven't found any trace of her," David said. "Trouble with finding bodies is that there's too many old shafts. One stick of dynamite dropped down after the corpse makes it look like any other abandoned mine. Nobody keeps records on how deep they are, and you can't search them all anyway."

He shook his head. "Sometimes a bloke will go down after setting off explosives and find bones in the rubble. They blow again real quick to cover up the bones. Then they just bore another shaft on the other side of the vein."

"Why would they cover up something like that?" I asked.

Bones uncovered that deep, he explained, most likely were ancient specimens. Only archaeologists would be interested in them but the police couldn't tell just by looking.

"Mining stops so they can investigate," David said. "No telling how long that would last. Most people can only afford to work one claim at a time, and an interruption like that would break them."

At the time, I had been chilled by the haste with which death was dismissed. But it's too easy for anyone who hasn't lived on the edge of survival to judge others who do.

Noodling

COOBER PEDY'S OPAL FIELDS had more to offer than opportunities to die early and a chance at lifelong wealth. People who noodled the slag heaps could find a souvenir, unearth enough to cover their living expenses, or hit that one big chunk that would pay off their car.

Graham, Marie's brother-in-law, noodled as a hobby. One of the most enjoyable parts of his visits were the hours he spent out in the fields sifting through the dross. He offered to take me along; everyone else wanted to avoid the dirty work.

We bumped over the fields in the company car Graham had borrowed for his visit. He was careful to avoid open shafts, especially as he had already knocked the tailpipe off by backing into a rock.

He parked beside a few fresh piles. We clambered up the tiny mountains, sinking past our knees and sliding back in powdery avalanches. Sunglasses to protect the eyes, a filter mask to protect the lungs, and a sifting pan were our only tools. Scooping up a dish of dirt, we swirled the grit into the wind and examined the remains for brittle color.

To stay clear of each other's billowing dust clouds, we worked on separate piles. Often I paused to look out across the desert. The solitary work, the wind like a rustling companion, and the panorama of empty plains created a quiet peace. Any opal we found would be a bonus. The real reason to noodle was to experience the vast silence and stillness between the horizons.

By the time we returned to the house, we were coated in fine white dust. Graham stored my pickings in a jar. Large pieces of opal would crack if allowed to dry, so the jar was filled with water. Lustrous bars of lime and candied apple sparkled in the crystal fire opal.

The area's long history, all of the intense labor required to fetch opal from the earth, and every tattered thread of cruel desire had been distilled into an old honey jar. The grit under my nails was the only evidence of opal's true cost.

Burgers and Donuts

IN THE EVENINGS as we cooked and ate and cleaned up, I fielded questions on American culture. Marie wanted to know about foods that were common in the US. This was long before the revolution that turned the nation against packaged and processed foods toward whole, organic, sustainable, crunchy, hippy soothing raw goodness.

But among people like Marie and David who travelled often, food was always of interest. What was good? What was gross? And, because humans are fascinated by the absurd, gross foods always sparked fascination and disgust in equal measures.

Marie asked first for detailed directions on brewing iced tea. The beverage, I discovered during my journey, fascinated Aussies and Brits alike. It seems that they brewed the tea as if making a hot cup or two and then refrigerated the liquid, resulting in a drink that was too bitter. I shared the secrets of cold brewing, sun brewing, and other tricks before Marie moved on to what Yanks ate for dinner.

"Hamburgers, right?" she asked.

Although I was reluctant to destroy all that international marketing by the omnipresent burger chains, I steered toward more realistic fare.

"More like steak and potatoes, I guess," I said. "Although we eat a lot of chicken and fish now. Healthy stuff. You know."

"And what do you eat for breakfast?"

"Coffee and donuts or a bowl of cereal, usually."

"Yeah, donuts," she said. "I've heard about them. What are they?"

I had seen a display of donuts at the bakery just the previous day. By then I had picked up some of the language differences, so I hadn't been surprised to see that donuts were called cakes. Gas was petrol, propane was gas, asphalt was bitumen, breakfast was breakies, and donuts were cakes.

"Those round thingies we saw at the bakery," I said. "The ones with the holes in the middle."

"Cakes?" she asked. "You eat *cakes* for breakies?"

"Oh, they're not made with cake batter."

"Are they the kind with icing and sprinkles or just plain?"

Perhaps she thought there was hope yet.

"Both, really," I said. "Depends on the person."

She grimaced. I told her it was patriotic to jumpstart the day with caffeine and sugar. I countered that their pastries were too rich. Aussies tended to favor an afternoon break that consisted of tea with some type of baked goody laden with cream. Sharing in that daily ritual always upset my stomach.

Then Marie asked the inevitable, and it was my turn to cringe. She wanted to know if I had experienced Vegemite. The spread, beloved in every corner of the country, was the most repulsive and foul mess in the history of culinary malpractice. The smell was enough to scare off the mentally balanced: think yeasty, moldy, fetid...kind of like socks that have been stuffed inside rubber sneakers and left to molder in a hot locker for a few months.

When it had been offered to me in a hostel in Sydney, the funky odor hadn't put me off. Cheese could be pretty stinky and it was great, right? So I actually wanted to try this thing called Vegemite. But I wasn't entirely without survival instincts. Having been warned about its strong flavor, I spread a tiny amount on a corner of toast.

I swear before all the gods that the Vegemite never actually touched my tongue. When the paste hit the roof of my mouth, the odor pushed up into my nose and sparked a bar brawl. The spectators had burst out laughing.

The main ingredients, according to the label, were yeast extract, salt, malt extract, vegetable extract, and vitamin B. Sounded healthy enough. The flavor was mostly salty and should have been innocuous.

But something blasphemous underlay the brine, something unnatural that no human being should ingest.

A few months later someone talked me into trying Promite, supposedly made with similar ingredients but with an animal product, perhaps marrow, added to the mix. My host swore it was not as bad for just that reason.

She lied.

Krispy Kreme

THURSDAY EVENING, I planned a fun adventure for my new friends in Coober Pedy. I walked over to the bakery alone and purchased all the donuts/cakes they had left. The plan was to rise early, brew coffee (even though instant was the only option), and fete my hosts with a Yankee meal.

Sandra, another of the family's relatives, discovered the purchase. She said that if anyone knew the donuts were in the house, they would be scooped up for dessert that evening. We hid the pastries in a cabinet behind the gas heater.

The hiding place was effective but turned out to have been a poor choice. The cabinet was too warm, and by morning the icing had oozed to the bottom of the bag. I prepared plenty of toast to pad those delicate Aussie stomachs and arranged the half-melted goodies on a platter.

Everything was laid out on the table with napkins. I bypassed the silverware Aussies used for pastries to encourage the full experience, which included eating with their fingers. At the first sight of the gooey mass, Marie moaned.

"Cor, no," she said.

"You have to try just one," I said.

"I have tried the bloody things and I bloody well know how they taste."

"They taste better in the morning. Come on, you don't have to drink coffee."

Sadly, Sandra was the only soul bold enough to indulge. She nodded her head a few times and wrinkled her brow whenever she bit into the donut. She eventually said it was all right but that she wouldn't do it again.

I, however, suffered a grave disappointment. The pastries were made of a heavy cake dough and had been baked instead of fried. I described the light, fluffy texture of a Krispy Kreme sugar donut, a delight only available east of the Mississippi River, to my nauseated audience.

"Each bite," I rhapsodized, "collapses down to a small, chewy bit with fresh glaze crumbling off the edges. They're so light you have to eat at least two."

"Two!" Marie cried. "No wonder all you Yanks die of heart failure. Bloody lot of pigs, you are!"

Dingo Fence

A SOLO DAY TRIP took me to the dingo fence. The barrier began in Surfers' Paradise, Queensland and didn't stop until it hit the Great Australian Bight near Western Australia. That's 5,600 kilometers of wooden posts and wire stretched between the horizons.

The fence protected the expansive sheep ranches in the southern states from Australia's largest wild predator. Poisoned bait and traps beleaguered the point. A rough maintenance track ran along the north side, so I parked the car and started walking.

When a white object caught my eye, I hunkered down to take a closer look. My peripheral vision caught the movement of many large animals barreling right at me. Dingoes! Adrenaline flooded my muscles. My hand groped for the knife but it was in the car. I was going to be ripped apart by a rabid pack of dogs!

I needed a weapon. Rocks of any useful size were oddly absent but I did have a rather large camera strapped around my neck. Before I died, I could bash in a few furry, slavering heads!

I jumped to my feet with the camera in one fist. As I turned to face my attackers, I saw only a mob of kangaroos. The large grey females and the even larger red males froze. As I clicked off a few shots, the lead roo blew loudly and stomped the ground. Tails flumping, they angled around me and disappeared into the distance.

Lady Emu

SAFELY ENSCONCED ON THE SOUTH SIDE of the fence—the dingo-free side—I continued my walkabout. At some point I descended into a dry streambed. The next time I poked my head up over the banks, a clutch of emus was padding along the fence. The father led four juveniles through the bush on their hunt for food.

Their long plumes rippled like silk and their bald heads were periscopes in a sea of dust. The female spent most of the year on her own turf; during breeding season, she entered the male's territory long enough to lay eggs on a site he had prepared. Then she whisked away and left dad with the incubation and childrearing chores.

I was much like that emu mother. I was in my late twenties and had turned down two marriage proposals already. Granted, the proposals weren't the kind you take seriously. The first had come during a blind date. After bar hopping—an activity I had never enjoyed, and one I particularly didn't enjoy that evening seeing as how bar food wasn't an acceptable substitute for dinner—we returned to his place.

Because he was a city dweller who hadn't found it necessary to fix his car the last time it had stopped running, I had driven us around all evening. I never drank if I was going to get behind the wheel but my date had consumed plenty of alcohol. If he had hoped to end the evening with a tipsy companion, he had effectively reversed the plan and ended up drunk himself.

At that point, it was pretty clear that there would be no second date. To me, anyway. He apparently felt differently.

When I pulled up, I left the motor running to signal that I wasn't going to go inside. Perhaps desperate to salvage the evening, he remained in the passenger's seat chattering, and chattering...and chattering. Nearly two hours later, he was still ensconced in the passenger's seat, I had to pee like a racehorse, and the gas gauge was dangerously low.

For the final forty-five minutes, he had talked about marriage—how much he wanted to be married, how ready he was for that next stage of life, and how one lucky lady with wit and intelligence and beauty (insert googly-eyed and earnest gazes deep into my eyes here) could find herself whisked into a frothy cloud of wedding-day bliss.

The guy was so desperate he came off as borderline batty. No way was I going to go inside to use the restroom and find my escape blocked by more chatter. But I couldn't march around to the other side of the car and physically eject him.

Finally I convinced him that, despite the sorrow parting would cause us both, it was imperative that I leave. We could get together the next evening for the triumphant moment that would spin his world the right way.

By the time I zoomed away, the car was on fumes and my watery backlog was causing painful cramps. Even though I was in the heart of Washington, DC, the gas stations were all closed. The trip home would cover nearly thirty miles on the freeway, not a place any woman wanted to run out of gas in the dark, quiet hours of the morning.

After a long search down streets I'd never driven before, I finally located an open filling station. I pumped enough gas to get home and then shot around the back of the building for the restroom.

Unfortunately, someone with bigger problems than mine had decided to camp inside. An excruciating fifteen minutes passed before the attendant finally roused the squatter. It might have taken another eight minutes to empty my bladder.

So, that was the first marriage proposal.

The second came at a party when I met a guy from the UK whose student visa was about to run out. He asked me (and probably every other woman at the party) if I would marry him so he could stay in the country. He said we could be roommates, which would save me a lot of money; after the requisite number of years or whenever he wanted to go home again, we could divorce. I turned him down.

I would later receive a third proposal from a traveler I met in Australia. He was a gay man who wanted desperately to move to the US to be with his boyfriend. He offered me cash, a few thousand dollars...US dollars, he was quick to point out, not the weaker Australian dollars. I turned him down, too.

That lady emu, who got what she needed while maintaining her independence, was my kind of bird.

God's Girlfriend

EVEN A DUST STORM THAT DROWNED Coober Pedy beneath a crimson wave couldn't dampen the weekend festivities. Every Friday night was disco night. The cafeteria of the Desert Cave, the world's only underground four-star hotel, hosted the rave.

People had talked about it all week. In a town where grinding work filled every hour and living conditions were basic, the gathering offered a bright spot. But, as with everything else in the Outback, the facilities were makeshift at best.

A mirrored ball dangled forlornly from the ceiling and the long tables had been shoved against the walls to create a dance floor. Despite the bare atmosphere, the bar was strangled by enthusiastic patrons.

Marie enjoyed her usual glass of Irish cream, I imbibed bourbon and cola, and David saved the Australian economy by slugging back endless beers.

"That's God," Marie said.

She pointed her cigarette at a small fellow in a dark suit and a precisely knotted tie. His crisp shirt, a single spot of white blazing amid everyone else's grubby clothes, shone as brightly as his lacquered shoes. His eyes swept the crowd with the smug confidence of a lord surveying his manor.

"He owns Coober Pedy," Marie said. "At least, he acts like he does. This hotel is his, and while they were excavating, he pulled heaps of opal from the ground. No one knows how much but it was enough to have paid off this bloody palace and let him retire. I've heard he made six million, mostly tax free. Sold under the table, you know."

She waved vaguely at a quiet blond seated at the end of our table.

"That's God's girlfriend," she said. "Not really his *girlfriend,* mind, but he's obsessed with her. She just wants to be friends."

A man I had decided was God's bodyguard, a threatening fellow who bulged in all the wrong places, placed a drink in front of the girlfriend. God waved a round of drinks around and within a few minutes the guard had fetched another for the blond. She objected that two were enough but the glass joined the others.

After ten minutes and two more rounds, I opened my mouth and out popped, "What about us, then?"

Somewhere in a head grown fuzzy with liquor and loud music floated the notion that God was rude not to include us in his benevolence. After all, David tended the hotel's lounge bar, Marie had worked at the front desk, and we were all as chatty as could be expected. What friendly employer wouldn't shout his pals a round?

The bodyguard conferred with God, I flashed my winsome smile, and a new round of drinks hit the table. According to Marie, that was the most impressive thing I accomplished while in Coober Pedy.

After the music and the spasmodic dancing got to be too much, we headed to the Anzac club. The meeting place drew veterans and their friends. A wood-burning stove blasted the interior with hellish heat. Rickety tables on the edge of collapse somehow supported the leaning weights and pounding fists.

Invectives shouted across the room with a wink and a nod greeted every newcomer but the bravado and joviality were a bit thick. A creeping desperation bowed every back as if the dust days had eroded any hope. In the corner, a young woman played darts as surreptitiously as possible. She missed the board more often when she felt the casual scrutiny of a bored gaze.

After a quick drink we left for home, subdued by the atmosphere. Only Marie spoke, muttering "losers" under her breath.

Snack Food

THE NEXT MORNING brought the International Day parade, a celebration of the community formed by all the world's nations. The parade was led by a group of indigenous people followed by representatives of various nationalities, each carrying a flag or banner. The Aboriginal flag consisted of a field of black for the people, a block of red for the earth, and a yellow circle at the middle for the sun.

Inside the civic hall, vendors pedaled their wares. It seemed as if the whole town was crammed inside. At one table an Aboriginal woman displayed paintings, crafts and artwork made by local clans. A plate of larvae, the witchetty grubs that had provided nomadic tribes with an easy source of protein, were also on display.

The creatures were huge. Their overstuffed bodies made them look like maggots on steroids. A shiny black head and a satiny white skin prevented them from being too repulsive. A nervous man who looked like a college professor waggled his finger above the plate.

"Excuse me," he said to the vendor. "May I borrow one of these...things to show my wife?"

"Yeah," she said. "You can even try one."

Try? As in eat? Eek! Was I ever excited. But hesitant. I picked up a witchetty and stroked its smooth skin. Thin Man used the tip of a pencil to coax a second grub onto his portfolio. He meticulously straightened the larvae, poking and prodding until it was a fat, placid exclamation mark against the maroon leather. He maneuvered through the crowd with the folio thrust away from his body as if the grub was radioactive.

"You want to try that one?" The vendor smiled eagerly.

"Uh...yeah, I think so," I said. "Maybe in a minute."

I returned the grub to the plate and wandered down the table. I fingered the painted rocks and tried to pluck up my courage, overcome cultural taboos, or conquer whatever had stopped me from merrily grinding up this new treat. Then I found myself staring at a mass of wiggling legs atop another plate.

Ants. *Huge* ants. The plate had been smeared with something sticky and dozens of ants had been stuck upside-down in the goo. Their brown abdomens were so distended they shone red.

Just for a second I thought of my grandfather. Pappy had been a special man, warm and generous with a wry sense of humor. He had given my brother and I chewing tobacco that we had promptly swallowed, had taught us how to smoke and use dangerous power tools, and generally had encouraged us to drive his son bonkers.

I had idolized him. When on a passing whim he had told me to eat an ant, I had immediately devoured the unfortunate insect. My brother, older and wiser, had been too suave to voluntarily eat bugs. So Pappy had sliced open strawberries and grapes with his pocket knife, shoved captives into the juicy coffins, and fed Richard the fruit.

"So what are these?" I asked the vendor.

There I went again. Opening my damn mouth.

"Honey ants," she said. "They're sweet. Want to try one?"

Honey ants collected nectar and stashed their cache inside special ants. As the colony's food source, these living storage tanks were protected deep underground where they dangled from the ceilings of their homes. In times of plenty, the storage ants could become so engorged that if they fell, they would burst. Sounds yummy, right?

"Umm...OK," I said. "What do I do?"

The American sweet tooth triumphed again. Besides, if I seriously intended to eat an enormous maggot, what harm could a little ant do? Anyway, the ants were much smaller than the grubs and therefore less threatening.

"Just pop it in your mouth," she said. "The honey is in the big sack in back."

"Do I have to eat the head?"

I felt relieved when she said no. Gingerly I removed a frantic ant from the trap. My concern about injuring the creature was silly because I was about to eat it. I popped the abdomen off with my teeth and my mouth filled with a sweet, runny liquid that tasted like honey.

"Hey, that's good!"

Discarding the head and thorax, I noticed that half the ants were missing their sacs but all were still waving their many legs. Only the vendor's beaming smile quelled my guilt. Which meant that I was ready to try a grub. Had I not just eaten an ant and really enjoyed it? I squeezed through the crowd, eager now to chow down before all the witchetties were snapped up.

"OK," I said. "What do I do now?"

"Just pick it up by the head and have a go."

Akk! Raw? *Alive?*

"Do I have to eat the head?" I asked.

What was this thing about eating heads? Why was it OK to eat everything else, including the icky bowels...and genitalia, come to think of it...but not the brains?

It wasn't about the brains or the limbs. A policeman once assured me that it was no big deal if someone found an arm or leg lying around. Most of the time the victim was still alive and quite happy without that pesky extra body part.

Finding a decapitated head was different. The face was the location of a human's identifying features. Removing the head from a corpse normally was the work of an extremely disturbed mind.

But we're talking about a witchetty grub.

With a nervous grin, I lifted the worm high. Around me, the crowd leaned forward in anticipation. When the grub touched my tongue, it grabbed on with its many feet. I resisted the urge to spit it out.

I snipped off the head thinking that this one, at least, enjoyed a quick death. As I chewed, a warm custard squirted across my tongue. The custard tasted faintly salty and a bit of grit squeaked between my teeth. Then the perfect mouthful was on its way down. Thin Man returned, shoveled his captive off the portfolio, and startled when I placed the beady head on the plate.

Much better than Vegemite.

As Bad as All That

AS DAVID DROVE US to Sunday brunch, teenagers slouched along the dirt sidewalk in Coober Pedy's business district. Sullen, defensive, and busily glancing about in defiance of everything and nothing, they cruised through the haze kicked up by passing cars.

For some reason, they really stood out from the rest of the people trotting along the sidewalk. I couldn't quite put my finger on what had drawn my attention until Marie glanced over.

"Tourists," she said.

"How can you tell?" I asked.

"They aren't dusty."

Of course.

As we ate, David offered to accompany me to Max's place, a cave just outside town in which an older fellow had set up house. Lots of people in Coober Pedy lived underground in dugouts, spaces they had carved out of the rock. But Max was a bit of a personality and had set himself up inside a natural cave.

Once we returned to the house and took care of a few things, David jangled his keys and waved me toward the door.

"Oh, I can go by myself," I said. "I'm sure you're sick of hauling me around by now."

"You don't want to go alone," he said.

"Max is an old lecher," Marie said with a wink.

"Harmless," David added, "but annoying. And I know how Yankee women are! You'll pop him one if he pats your bum!"

On the trip over, David told me a little about Max. He, like so many other Australians, allowed travelers to stay in the spare room or camp outside of his cave. Max did this so often that his home had become a pretty regular stop for people from around the world.

When the car ground to a halt, I tumbled out first. Other travelers gave us a quick nod as they continued stuffing their 4WD truck with an assortment of packs and swags. Surely Max wouldn't dare grope or grab with so many others around.

Then he rounded the fender. He was quite a bit older and stooped from age or the harsh living conditions or perhaps just a life of hard labor. At any rate, he wasn't exactly spry. Nevertheless, he shuffled toward me at top speed with his splayed hands reaching for my breasts.

His brazen approach was so shocking that I froze. David knew just what to do. He had circled around the rear of the car to stand behind me. When he called out a greeting, the shuffling slowed. Max's face, darkened by sun, wind and dirt, seemed baffled. Then he linked my appearance to that of his neighbor. His hands dropped and twitched disconsolately at his sides.

A mere dollar bought the privilege of touring his cave. *Road Warrior* had been filmed nearby, and props salvaged from the set were displayed in the cave. A clothesline strung across the hallway dangled bras and knickers of every conceivable size and color, which Max claimed were gifts from grateful young women. In the bedroom, names and dates had been painted by a host of visitors across the ceiling.

"All these names," David whispered, "are people who lost their virginity here."

I rolled my eyes and snorted.

A few months later I discovered that PBS had visited the cave. The film crew had neglected to memorialize the knickers and had explained the ceiling collage as a record of travelers who had stopped by. PBS has always shown impeccable taste.

Taking Flight

I BADE FAREWELL TO MY HOSTS and continued my journey north. By that point, I had given the car a name. During my time in Adelaide, the motor had been stripped down and rebuilt. The work had been done under the supervision of Mary's neighbor, a mechanic who ran a traveler's garage out of his home.

By the end of our efforts, the motor growled with comforting strength. The car was christened Chugger in honor of its solid performance. Which did not mean that the Ford was perfect. A number of flaws that would have been insignificant in a city held potentially dangerous consequences in the Outback.

Soon after leaving Coober Pedy, the latch on the hood broke. Chugger happened to be flying along at a fast clip, which meant that the hood flew up and smashed against the windshield. Although the roof took most of the impact and saved the glass, I was suddenly blind.

Since highways in Australia's interior were narrow strips of asphalt barely large enough for two lanes of traffic, veering even a little to either side risked a collision with an oncoming vehicle or a dangerous loss of traction. Jamming on the brakes while blinded wasn't the best option as I wouldn't be able to manage the skid.

In the few seconds of leeway allowed by the straightness of the road, I found a safe way to react. I rolled down the window and stuck my head out. I still couldn't see much but the edge of the road became a guide that allowed me to slow safely. I pulled off, used a bungie cord to tie down the hood, and headed out again.

Once I was convinced that the bungie cord would hold, I relaxed and enjoyed the journey. Flocks of galahs raked the ground for tubers and roots. As Chugger approached, they rose in waves like a fluttering shawl. Their rouge breasts shone almost crimson in the long afternoon light, becoming a dirty white banner as the flock turned its grey backs and wings to the sun.

Sulphur-crested cockatoos were much larger and much noisier. Whenever I disturbed them, the flocks exploded into the sky to scream their protests. Hawks and eagles feasted on carrion. Whenever their meal lay in the road, the raptors waited until the last moment to fly off. As the car bore down, seemingly too fast for them to escape, they caught the updraft off the grill and wheeled straight over the roof.

My new life allowed for plenty of time to notice such special moments. Somewhere deep inside, my wings began to unfurl.

Camp Tunes

THE MEMORIES OF expansive wild spaces were driven from my mind one dismal evening. That night would be the last I voluntarily passed in a caravan park. Things were already looking pretty miserable because the trunk had leaked during the rains in Coober Pedy. The wool blankets that were so critical to keeping me warm during the cold desert nights had turned soggy.

Making due with what I had, I lugged the propane lantern into the tent to capture a bit of heat. The blue flame guttered and died before my fingers had thawed. The tank was empty and, I would later discover, I had no skill with managing the odd netlike bag that corralled the flame. Instead of having the jet burn properly, I melted one bag after the other before exchanging the lantern for a much messier and smellier kerosene version.

For that night, then, I had to suffer clammy blankets and layers of clothing that wadded up every time I moved inside the sleeping bag. I had just snuggled into my bulky cocoon when a little girl paused on the tiny patch of ground outside my temporary home.

"Mummy!" she shouted. "Whose tent is that?"

Her mother ran across the compound to shush her.

"Why is that tent in our space?" the girl shrilled.

"It's not, honey," Mama said.

"Who would sleep in there?" the girl wondered, sounding almost offended. "It's so small!"

The child, you should know, had arrived in a caravan. Said caravan consisted of four trucks, each of which hauled a small trailer. The trailers had unfolded into enormous bivouac tents, the kind used by natural catastrophe response teams. The front portion of each tent functioned as a living room while the rear was divided into two smaller bedrooms. Parents in one space, kids in the other.

So the girl had palatial quarters, especially compared to my pup tent, which would only have slept two if the campers were intimately acquainted. Adding to the child's comfort were folding tables, throne-like folding chairs, portable two- and four-burner stoves, five-gallon cook pots, a gas-powered mini refrigerator, an entire box of spices, wash buckets and gas lampposts, folding cots with mattresses, and plenty of blankets that surely weren't soggy.

Darkness fell only in other parts of Australia; the grass verge in the caravan park was lit up like Times Square. Sleep was a long time coming because my neighbors' household goods included a radio. They chattered over the music for quite some time. After a few beers, they whipped out a recording of their favorite camping tunes.

"Put another log on the fire!" they howled.

"Put a la la na, la-da la da," they fizzled out for the next line.

Then a moderate form of silence fell while one or two people who actually knew the words sang the next lines.

"Put another log on the fire!" they roared at the chorus.

I distinctly remember thinking, *I'm in hell.* Americans might be ugly but Aussies are loud.

Things finally seemed to be dying down when footsteps again approached my tent. Two voices conversed about the fuse box near my feet. The fellow who had rented the powered site across from the rabble-rousers was having trouble with his electrical supply. The park owner showed him which fuse to flip if it blew again.

"I don't understand why I should be having a problem," the camper said.

"The lines aren't set up for a high load," the owner said. "If you draw too much power, it'll trip off."

With complete sincerity the man said, "But I only have a light, a heater, and a black-and-white TV!"

Uluru

AFTER MORE THAN A MONTH in the relentlessly flat and open desert, confronting the mass of stone standing at the midpoint of the country was magical. This was the site known to many as Ayer's Rock for the European explorer who had reported its existence to the newcomers. Aboriginal tribes had known it for much longer and called it Uluru.

For the Aborigines, the rock was sacred. Their lives had been lived around it in the nearly featureless desert, so the looming mound was clearly something special. As I drove closer, light shifted and played across its surface. All thought washed cleanly away; my brain wasn't big enough to accommodate anything other than wonder.

Tourists had the option to climb to its summit. From the parking lot, the journey looked neither high nor difficult. But a short distance up the slope was an area called Chicken Rock. At this point the route suddenly became quite steep and many hikers turned back.

The erosion caused by passing feet had worn a thin pink ribbon onto the surface. The surrounding stone was scaly and pocked like a red moon. Large flakes of rock clinging to the slopes hid deep shadows. Hundreds of wooly brown caterpillars humped frantically up the gritty sides, apparently as determined to reach the summit as their human companions.

After I had realized that my journey would take me to Australia, I had tried to train physically. A backpack loaded with forty pounds of gear was kept in the car so that my lunch hour could be spent walking with the pack. But a few weeks of training followed by months of walking without a pack had done nothing for my fitness. Soon the climb left me puffing and aching.

I crawled away from the traffic to rest near a father and his son. The young teen's face was flushed with exertion and he seemed distraught.

"Don't worry," his father murmured. "We'll go slow. You'll be fine."

"You see those?" I pointed to the caterpillars. "If they can climb Uluru, so can I!"

The teenager broke out in a genuine smile. We found our breath and continued up together.

Reaching the top made all the effort worthwhile. The view commanded a stunning expanse of the endless plains. The land was surprisingly green where hardy shrubs had found just enough to survive. The paved road was the only evidence of mankind.

As fellow hikers arrived, they celebrated having reached the top. Then someone said that we had completed only a third of the climb. After another trek up another slope, we stepped onto the top of Uluru.

The plateau was wide, so hikers spread out to explore. I found a quiet spot far from the others and again considered the view. The sides that fell away beneath my feet were rumpled like a sheet bunched on a line. Bird had made their nests in the recesses between the folds and launched themselves into the sky. The sun was hot but a cooling wind whisked the stone.

The magic of it filled my mind. The energy of the place, so ancient and rightfully sacred, moved through my heart. This was a small piece of what I had been seeking all my life, the connection that had been lost in the rush of workdays and the crush of traffic jams and the chaos of everyday chores. Separated from the crowds, I felt the first touch of peace.

An Education

EVENTUALLY I HAD TO REJOIN the flow of hikers on Uluru. A cairn noting the elevation, almost 3,000 feet, held a visitor's log. People crowded around and jumped in front of each other to write something of their own in the log. Frustration at those who took too long to leave a comment scratched the air.

The second a person had made their mark, had proven to themselves and to others that they had made the climb, they started the trip back down. The rush to mark off another line item on a list meant that they didn't truly live in the moment. I was as guilty as anyone else. I was, in fact, taking this journey hoping to find a new way to be in the world.

So, after scribbling my own note in the log, I wandered a different direction across the peak. In a puddle left by a recent rain lay a cluster of jelly-like balls. Each held a dark nuclei. I wondered if they were the eggs of an amphibian that stayed dormant until the rains. When I shared this with the father and son, the man swore he had seen a tiny fish dart through one of the other pools.

The return trip seemed more difficult than the climb. Fatigue and blisters took their toll. Despite the terrible heat, I was one of few hikers carrying water. Many people had died conquering Uluru, most from heat stroke or heart failure. Some had simply slipped and tumbled off the side. Lore claimed that the spirits who lived in the stone tired of people tromping on their roof and pushed them off.

That day had its share of near misses. My lens cap twirled off into space and I almost followed by lunging after it. A madman jogged down the steepest section with never a thought to the chain. Then a group of teenagers complained about how weak their legs had grown and scooted down on their butts. They roared when one passed wind.

"Did you fart? Who farted?" screamed one.

"I did," giggled another.

"You can't fart here! This is Uluru! It's...it's not allowed!"

"Yeah," agreed a third, "you can't shit on Uluru."

"But I did and I'm proud," proclaimed the guilty party. "I shitted upon Uluru!"

"No," I called out, "that's not right."

The sound of an adult's voice created sudden and complete silence. Into this void I launched my wisdom.

"You shat upon Uluru," I said. *"Shat,* past tense of *to shit.* I shit, I will shit, I shat, I have shat."

Storms of laughter rose from the girls. A fellow behind me muttered about how poorly children were educated these days and grinned.

A Wild Companion

AFTER MY STRENUOUS EXPLORATION of Uluru, I checked to see if Mighty Mouse had already eaten. Mighty Mouse was the rodent that had taken up residence in my car. For weeks I had been annoyed by the shredded wrappers and the food it gnawed through every night, which I felt compelled to throw out for fear of catching some strange mouse virus.

I was also worried it would chew the wiring in the car. I didn't need to be stranded hundreds of miles from the nearest roadhouse or small town because of a hungry rodent's misguided midnight snacks. Then I struck on a perfect solution.

I started leaving food out for the little guy. It was easier for the mouse to get what it needed and caused me much less worry. During my hike up Uluru, Mighty Mouse had helped itself to a crust of bread and a carrot end I'd left on the floor. How it survived the heat that built up inside the car, I'll never know. But the invisible pet made something of a companion for me even if I never did spot him.

The Locals

A SMALL COLLECTION OF SHOPS in nearby Yulara promised a hearty dinner. Although I didn't eat much in the roadhouses, the occasional grocery stores sometimes offered fresh foods...or, as was often the case, they offered packaged fare that was different than the potatoes and PB&Js that were my staples.

I pulled into a parking lot around dusk. As I locked the car, an Aboriginal fellow approached and asked if I was going to the store. The moment I said yes, he pressed a wad of bills into my hand.

"You buy BPs." He waved me on my way.

"Excuse me?" I asked.

His accent was thick so I wasn't sure exactly what he wanted.

"You buy BPs," he said. "Bring here. Por me."

None of the tribal languages contained the "f" sound, which further confused my ears. I looked at the wad of twenties uncertainly. Whatever he wanted wasn't cheap; almost a hundred dollars was crumpled in my fist. I shook my head and shrugged. And like anyone trying to break the language barrier, he tried speaking louder.

"BPs! You buy carton BPs!"

With that single additional word, the light shone through. He wanted a carton of cigarettes, and the brand was BP. Cigarettes ran over AU$40.00 a carton, which explained the large amount of money.

Of course, anyone might wonder why he didn't just walk over there and buy them himself. But the weeks I'd spent in Coober Pedy showed me an Outback that was rough with a lifestyle that was rougher. People got drunk on occasion and acted poorly. The heat alone was enough to drive people mad and make them do things they normally would never do.

I therefore assumed that he had been banned from the store at some point. Exactly why didn't matter to me. He was hundreds of miles from another grocery store and wanted cigarettes. I was heading there already, and it would cost me nothing to help.

"What kind?" I asked. "BPs?"

"BPs!" He smiled and nodded.

"Just one?" I asked.

"Carton BPs." He tapped the money. "Por me. Bring back."

And off I tottered on my mission of kindness. Oh, how good I felt. Oh, how wonderful it would be to hand this man his cigarettes and be on my way. Oh, what a warm and fuzzy hug I was giving myself!

The general store held the usual herds of travelers sweeping the shelves bare in a foraging frenzy. After weaving through them and picking enough to fill a hand basket, I approached the counter. The cashier rang up my total. I then said I needed cigarettes and requested a carton of BPs. The cashier looked confused.

"What brand?" he asked.

"BPs," I repeated, cocksure that a carton of cigarettes would appear at any moment.

The fellow behind me heard my Yank accent and leaned in to help. "Might you want Benson and Hedges?" he asked.

Surely this Aussie bloke knew what he was talking about.

"Yes!" I said. "I want Benson and Hedges."

I returned to the parking lot with the cigarettes in one bag and my groceries in another. The sun had set and the parking lot was dark. As I approached my car, the man stepped out and eyed my purchases suspiciously.

"I'm not sure I bought the right kind," I said as I opened the lighter bag. "But they must be close because—"

He was already walking away, muttering and throwing both hands into the air. Apparently I had bought the wrong brand.

"Wait!" I called. "Don't you at least want your change?"

He turned on his heel and stamped back, still muttering.

"I'm sorry—"

"V.B. V!B!" he yelled quite clearly. "V.B. beer, Victoria Bitter!"

Oops.

Although the man tried to send me back for the beer, I declined. Alcoholic beverages were allowed on Yulara only as a special concession for tourists. Otherwise the area was a land claim and, as on most other land claims, the tribal council had forbidden the sale of alcohol to native people.

I wasn't ready to judge someone's intention for buying alcohol but I also wasn't about to break the law. He took his change, the unwanted cigarettes, and went his way. I got into the car and went mine but not without thinking for a very long time about this particular clash of cultures into which I had unwittingly stepped.

Mapping the Wilderness

THE POPULATION SO FAR INTO the Never Never was, to state the obvious, sparse. So few roads had been carved through the region that I navigated using a map of the nation. The map wasn't even a proper road map; instead, I used the folded insert that had come in a special edition of *National Geographic.*

The long dirt roads known as spurs, most of which could only be accessed using a four-wheel-drive vehicle, were marked, which made the map detailed enough. Solitary towns were scattered like knuckle bones across the Outback. Occasionally the town consisted of two or three shops but often they were lonely roadhouses dropped among the mulga.

Every morning when I unfolded the map across the hood of the car, the emptiness was a reminder of everything I had come to this country to find: solitude. Wilderness. And somewhere in that vast void, myself.

The distances I tracked between where I was (always in a vague, "around here" kind of way) and the places I would go (often equally as vague but occasionally one of the towns) reminded me of the danger. Travel in a foreign country was always a challenge, and remote travel in a foreign country even more so. The boldness of a woman who chose to travel alone was—and to a large extent remains—a gender-specific risk layered atop the others.

My mother, in fact, had arranged to take pictures of me before I left. Although she wouldn't admit to her logic, I knew why. She wanted something to give to the police and rescue squads in case I disappeared. I thought of it as "the death photo" but spared her by not mentioning that until after my return.

All along the remote highways and even in the larger towns, pubs and roadhouses hung bulletin boards where travelers could post messages to each other. Many were missed connection notices; many more were requests for rides or offers to provide rides in exchange for sharing the cost of petrol.

Mixed in with these scraps of paper and index cards were full-page photocopies of missing persons. The pictures were often grainy from having been enlarged but they captured the personalities of individuals who had gone on vacation or looking for a job and disappeared. Their smiles, their expressions, and especially their eyes defined the ragged holes left in the lives of their loved ones.

I was, therefore, never far from these reminders. Any woman—whether she decides to travel alone, with friends, with a lover or spouse, or even when she journeys only from her car to her workplace or through a nearly empty parking lot—is never far from danger. A gaze that lingers or footsteps approaching from behind triggers her senses and tells her to beware.

These triggers and more required my attention during this journey. Every car that slowed on the highway after I had pitched my tent, every camper that pulled up next to my bivouac needed to be assessed. The hunter's skinning knife I had been given as a preteen, a heavy tool with a curved blade, lay beside my sleeping bag every evening.

It was intended only as a backup. As in daily life, a woman's wits have always been her best defense.

Temporary Companion

ALICE SPRINGS WAS LARGE for such a remote town. As such, it offered a great deal more selection in terms of groceries and other supplies. The services also made for a nice break; restaurants, cafes, and the tourist trade provided a short vacation from rough bush living.

A young British fellow (a Pommy, as the Aussies called them) asked me for directions to the post office. I was heading there myself, so we wandered around together until we'd found the correct building. After posting messages to assure our relatives that we weren't dead yet, we visited a local cafe.

Although I was far from the type of traveler who deliberately sought out other campsites in order to socialize, sharing a bit of time with other travelers now and then was soothing. I encountered few Americans during my trip, perhaps because I avoided most of the guided tours and tour buses.

No matter where my temporary companions hailed from, we held a singular and important element in common. We were curious about this country, we were sacrificing comforts and the known in order to experience a life that was fully alive. Many, of course, had flung themselves into this adventure only for the bragging rights or for the freedom it offered from everyday tedium.

Some—more than a few, really—had undertaken the journey with awareness. They were the kind of travelers I gravitated toward. They were the kind who fed me with their own understanding of my intent. They were comrades, and their stories have stuck with me to this day.

But, as the British fellow had discovered, intentions didn't always lead directly to success. He had started out with three friends, a shared car, and shared expenses. What had seemed logical and workable at home had rapidly descended into chaos. Incessant bickering over who was paying for what had split the group apart.

The others had bought out his share of the car so that he could travel on his own. His new plan had been to use the buses to get from town to town. Rather than board the public buses, he had been lured by the cheap package deals offered by tour operators.

For me, packaged tours were too sanitized. They would be an option only if no other way to access a certain area could be found. As it turned out, the British fellow was also not suited to exploring with a bunch of strangers.

"These bleeding bus tours," he groused, "are worse than the fights. Cramped in a tiny seat for hours next to people I don't even like! All for twenty minutes or an hour at the site."

"Must be pretty awful," I said. "I kinda feel sorry for you."

"Good," he said. "Because I feel sorry for me, too."

The best traveler, we agreed, had a sense of humor.

Aussie Fables

THE CONVERSATION WITH THE young Pommy turned to amusing Aussie quirks. We laughed over the fables told about the redback, a spider related to North America's black widow. While many pioneers had fallen prey to the tiny fiend, antivenin and the slow effects of the poison made it much less of a threat for modern travelers.

The danger had been raised to mythic proportions by the strange evolution of Australian toilets. When flush toilets had first become available, water closets had not been installed inside houses. Instead, they had been placed in additions with separate entrances that required homeowners to step outside to use the restroom.

The rooms were barely more than utility sheds that often were unheated. As with any infrequently used space, they sheltered various insects. The redback, which preferred to build messy snare webs beneath piles of junk, found a perfect habitat under the toilet seat.

Anyone who sat on the seat without first flipping up the lid to check for arachnid tenants risked being bitten on their butt, a blow that caused death by venom or embarrassment. The British fellow had been warned about the spiders but hadn't been told that they only haunted outdoor toilets.

"I was very cautious when I first arrived," he said with a grin. "My first night at the hotel, I shoved the bathroom door open so hard it crashed against the wall. I wanted to surprise any redbacks running about the floor."

"Did you see any?" I asked.

"No, but by that time I was so scared I was almost hyperventilating. I saw that strip, that paper band on the seat, what does it say?"

"Sanitized for your protection."

"Yes, something like that, but it didn't fool me one bit. I braced myself in the doorway, stretched out my leg and gave the toilet seat a mighty kick, expecting that an enormous, hairy spider would leap out and bite me. For a whole week I held my piss for hours so as not to have something assault my bum."

He looked a little embarrassed but was a great sport. Then, because my own sense of humor was a little mischievous and perhaps a little strange, I couldn't help but share another Australian fable.

"Have you heard about the drop bears?" I asked.

He shrugged, and my face took on a grave expression.

"Now there's another terrible bush peril," I said. "You know those fuzzy things that look like little bears?"

"Koalas," he said.

"Whatever. They live in trees and eat nothing but certain types of eucalyptus leaves."

He nodded.

"If it eats the wrong leaf," I said, "it gets all woozy and drunk. And sometimes the bear loses its grip and falls. Those drop bears may be small but they're very muscular and heavy. Every year some tourist is struck on the head by a falling drop bear and dies. So always look up."

For all I know, he still searches the trees for those elusive yet deadly drop bears.

Precious Gifts

USING ALICE SPRINGS AS A BASE, I explored the outlying region. Roads ran east and west of the town for a few hundred kilometers, and various natural areas were marked on the map. I camped for a night or two before moving to the next one; whenever I needed fresh food, a quick trip back to town resupplied the groceries.

One day I called an early halt to do laundry bush style. The sturdy hiking pants I had cut into shorts and the t-shirts that had become my daily uniform were washed in a bucket. Cleanliness was mostly about deodorizing and rinsing away the dirt; stains, especially those created by the red dust, simply wouldn't come out.

The cleanish items were then draped over a clothesline strung between the car and a nearby tree. While sun and wind plucked the moisture from my tiger-print bloomers, I attended to another regular chore, the call of nature.

Daylight hours usually demanded the most walking because the thin scrub didn't conceal much. At this pullover, a rocky outcropping sheltered my shiny cheeks from the neighboring trailer. Still, this most necessary of activities was perpetually annoying. No matter how deep the pit nor how widely I straddled the ground, my shoes were always sprinkled.

After I had freshened up, a couple in a camper invited me for tea and cookies. When they discovered that my propane stove had been abandoned and I was cooking over a fire, the elderly husband insisted on collecting my firewood. I was a woman, you see, and he didn't want me to hurt myself.

Then he ratcheted off into the desert on stiff legs. Although he was gone quite some time, he returned with barely a handful of kindling. The twigs were piled triumphantly beside the fire pit at my site. They then dug through their camper and presented me with a propane tank and stove they never used.

Their generosity was moving. Before this trip, I had gotten rid of many possessions to lighten a life that had felt pretty cluttered. Although I had always tried to give freely of my things and myself, in Oz I was flooded with gifts from strangers. Invitations, assistance, and a bit of free advice were only a few of the things offered without hesitation or expectation.

Even a hot mug of tea or coffee was more than just a beverage. It was an invitation to share an evening, to spend time completely absorbed in the lives of others with nothing due in return except a laugh or a pat on the back. I gradually understood that everything I had given, materially and spiritually, was being returned to me tenfold, a hundredfold.

Beautiful Sites with Beautiful Sights

DUSK WALTZED ARM IN ARM with the cold, and I lounged with the older couple around the fire. They had built the inferno Australian travelers seemed to prefer. Apparently the man—or perhaps his wife—had scavenged most of the available firewood before their effort to stack wood on my campsite.

On this bonfire they boiled a huge billy, a kettle or pot used to heat water, just to brew a few cups of tea. For some reason, I had expected the Aussies to be more conservation minded. The lack of urbanization in the desert should have made protecting their natural environment easier. But much of the land had already bent beneath herds of cattle and sheep.

Still, the desert held a particular and stunning beauty. The next morning brought proof of its powerful attraction. Unfortunately the proof arrived as I prepared to bathe using a portable shower bag. A swimsuit maintained my modesty while allowing access to all the little bits that needed attention.

Performing such a basic and personal task under the sky further connected me with the earth. Bushes were in flower, one a faint purple and the other pink; fuzzy golden wattle cushioned my feet against the red earth; and broken rock jittered through the ground like the bony spine of a flame dragon.

As I drenched my body and reached for the soap, a 4WD truck pulled up. The occupants, a young couple on holiday, honored me with more than one glance. People often checked out the gear of other travelers, especially those of other campers, so their curiosity didn't bother me.

The bus tour...now, that bothered me.

The coach parked about twenty feet away, close enough that lathering any part of my body except my head suddenly became an uncomfortably erotic exhibition. I stared down a few fish-like gapers as they shuffled slowly—too slowly—after the tour guide. Gathered at the other end of the bay, they gazed at the splendid outcropping I had commandeered for my toilet.

While they were (mostly) distracted, I scrubbed as discreetly as possible. Just as I raised the shower bag for a rinse, the group shuffled back to the vehicle. And up rumbled a second bus. The gawping commenced, I glowered again, and a few seconds were snatched to rinse and condition while they ogled the outcropping. Then a third bus arrived, forcing me to wait again.

Ah, the wonders of two-way radio.

Cradle Rocker

I RETURNED TO THE ALICE to purchase a didgeridoo, an Aboriginal wind instrument created when termites hollowed out a tree branch. The insides were often burned out, a painstaking process using embers, to remove loose wood. Kinks and curves enhanced the richness of the sound, and the best didgeridoos had a flare at the bottom that could disperse the sound.

Even though mine was straight, it produced a wonderful mellow tone. A rough sprinkling of sand overlay the white, red, brown and yellow bands painted on the outside. Musicians often accompanied the drone with click sticks, a modernized version of clap sticks or boomerangs.

In a pub that evening, I relaxed at a table by myself. An Aboriginal woman named Melody paused to chat and soon beckoned me to her table to meet her friends. They spoke Aboriginal creole, a mix of English and local tribal languages. Melody had been a teacher and a health counselor for the local tribes until her job had "gone down with the rain."

"Sss," she hissed between her teeth. "But I stay here, this my home. Not Alice, you know, but out, you know, outside."

She fixed me with a slow, easy grin.

"I no cradle rocker, neither!" she said. "I not born in hospital. I born over there."

She gestured at one wall, beyond which the Outback rolled across its vast expanse.

"I born in riverbed when dry, *sss.* My sons born here, too. They no cradle rocker either. I go back where I born when their time come. River dry then, too, *sss.*"

At some point, her friends left. She and I stayed on, talking about the desert and the town. I fetched drinks for both of us from the bar. When I returned, Melody asked for ten dollars.

"Sorry," I said. "I don't have ten dollars to spare."

"Five then," she said.

I shook my head. She sighed and rummaged through her pockets. After depositing a handful of condoms atop the table, she spread out the packets. Since I had no gift for her, she would offer a gift to me.

"Take one, be safe," she said. "You never know, you see handsome man."

I laughed and reached for one of the condoms.

"Wait," she said. "I pick for you. What color you like?"

"What colors do you have?" I asked.

"I had blue but now only black and white."

She cut her eyes sideways. I laughed and shook my head.

"Either," I said. "I like all the colors of the rainbow!"

She giggled and placed one finger decisively on a condom before pushing it in front of me.

"I give you black one," she said. "Everyone need black one at least once!"

Bloody Tourists

I DECIDED TO CAMP in a large parking bay that lay close to the Alice along the highway leading up from the south. The bay was popular for just that reason, and a few trailers at the edge of a stream looked as if they had been entrenched for weeks.

My first order of business was to stock up on firewood. A pit had been dug by a previous camper, leaving me only to round up half a dozen fairly large stones. The rocks would contain the fire, provide a shelf for the kettle, and retain heat long after the embers had retired.

Laying out my swag was the most demanding task. The cold desert nights required several blankets (which were now stored on the back seat to keep them dry), two sleeping bags, a tarp beneath the tent, and a foil blanket spread across the tent's floor. Even those layers weren't enough insulation, so my nightclothes were a swaddle of thermal underwear and sweats.

After all that fidgeting, it was simple enough to unfold a lawn chair and sink into a long communion with the landscape. With the typewriter precariously perched on the cooler, I used the daylight hours to update my journal. The edges of the paper had already yellowed and curled from the heat, and the first page of my handwritten notes had bleached away under the sun.

"Excuse me!" a voice called.

A woman charged across the clearing. Her idea of personal space was much narrower than my own, and she stopped just short of bulldozing me. I looked up at her with my hands still hovering over the typewriter keys.

"Can we share this space?" she asked. "There isn't another clear spot left."

"Sure," I said. "Come on over."

My residence had actually been erected some distance from the official boundaries of the parking bay. Travelers would continue to arrive until late into the night, and a little distance from the main cluster was always nice. However, after so many long evenings of solitude in a row, a bit of company before tucking in sounded appealing.

Although the woman and her companions were now free to settle in, she hadn't moved. She loomed there eying me expectantly. We gazed at each other as the seconds ticked by and my welcoming smile became strained. Finally she spoke.

"You'll have to move these things," she said.

She flapped her hands to indicate my cooler, my chair, my typewriter, myself. I must have looked like a fish surprised by a harpoon because she offered an explanation.

"It's a tight fit," she said firmly, "and we want to park there."

Her finger snapped out to indicate the opposite side of the fire pit. I didn't understand why she had chosen that narrow strip of ground over the more spacious clearing in which she stood but all campers had their habits. After I obliged, one of the two Kombis squeezed around the rocks. The valves rattled a final time as the motor wheezed to a thankful stop.

I had just moved all my things back into their original positions when the woman informed me of my next chore.

"You'll have to move your car," she said.

My eyebrows leapt.

"We park side by side," she said, "and your car's in the way."

She folded her arms across her chest. Surely she knew that this was one command too many, for she bristled like a sea urchin that nevertheless expected to have its way. I strangled my anger and managed to sound somewhat calm.

"And where," I asked, "do you suggest I move it?"

"Over there."

Her hand flapped at the craggy landscape.

"I'm afraid," I said politely, "my car doesn't have four-wheel drive."

"Well, just move that, then." Flap, flap, this time at my tent. "If you move that," flap, "you can move the car there," flap, "and we can park there."

Her face was awash in smug pleasure at the precision of her logic.

"Darling," called the second driver. "Just move and I'll park there."

"Where?" she asked.

"There. Where you're standing."

"I don't want to park here. I want to park over there."

One spiny finger jabbed at a patch of ground that really wasn't any less rocky than any other patch of ground.

"There's no room there," the husband called. "If you'll just move I'll park where you're standing."

"But I don't want to park here." Any easy flapping had been long dismissed in this battle of wills. "I want it over there!"

Over in the other van, the one that accompanied the urchin and her spouse, sat another couple. The driver gripped the wheel and his unblinking eyes were locked dead ahead. The passenger drooped against the window frame as if they had done this a thousand times before and would a thousand times again.

And people wondered why I traveled alone.

The Clever Man

AFTER A FEW DAYS, my explorations took me to the Pitchi Richi Sanctuary. The outdoor cultural and heritage museum displayed agricultural equipment and water tanks that had been used during Australia's colonization. An outdoor gallery featured the sandstone sculptures of artist William Ricketts, and the grounds served as a bird sanctuary for many wild species.

The small garden planted in front of the main building included the spectacular Stuart's Desert Pea. The vine produced an elongated flower that resembled a pea pod. When the pod split open, it revealed crimson petals and a large black bulb called a boss at the center. An Aboriginal story said the petals were the blood of a family that had been murdered as they slept.

The museum's best offering was a demonstration of boomerang and spear throwing, bullwhip cracking and didgeridoo playing by a man named Billy. He dug damper, a type of unleavened bread, fresh from the pit oven. After he had sawed off the burned crust, the sweet, thick slices were dressed with melted butter. When the water boiled, he threw a handful or two of loose tea into the billy. A sharp rap on the side of the bucket sank most of the leaves.

"Some old jackaroos," he said, "swear you can clear the leaves by swinging the billy over your head. 'Course, none of them jackaroos would show me, exactly, and I never did have a mind to douse myself with boiling water."

During his lecture, traditional items were passed around. A nulla nulla, a fighting stick, had been fashioned from the ironwood tree. The tool was also used for digging or pounding food. A sharp flint inserted in the end could have been used in battle but more often had sliced open game. The carcass would have been thrown onto the fire whole to singe the hair, and the blade wouldn't have been used until the meat was partially cooked.

The lecture ended and most of the audience left. A young American hung back with me to talk a bit more with Billy. After a moment, the docent moved to the base of the tree. He fished through a tattered box and produced a pair of slippers woven from human hair and feathers.

"You can look," he told me, "but only the bloke here can touch. These are male objects. Even though you're not tribal they have such a strong curse that I'd be afraid for you if you broke tradition."

"I respect that," I said.

"I keep these hidden so that tribal women won't see them. These belonged to a *karadji* man, the fellow responsible for enforcing punishments handed down by the elders. If an Aboriginal women saw these she'd probably run away screaming."

He tossed one to the ground. Then he rolled his foot atop the slipper and shifted his weight fully onto the shoe. As he gingerly peeled it from the ground, he waved at the dust.

"It leaves hardly any imprint," he said. "Soon the wind will sweep even that away. The victim never knows where the clever man came from or where he went because there were never any tracks."

"Were these shoes ever used?" the American man asked.

"Several killings were performed in these shoes."

"May I ask how?"

"The *karadji* man doesn't always spear the criminal," Billy said. "He might play with the fellow, leave signs that he'd been there like move his things or take something and return it another night. The victim knows he could have been killed but the clever man left it for another day."

"Why would he do that?" the American asked.

"Being stalked makes the victim obsessed with death. Many just waste away or meet with an 'accident' of their own design."

"What sorts of crimes are punishable by death?"

"Lots of things. Rape, murder, if you hurt a child or molest it...stuff like that."

"Is that the only type of punishment?"

"Oh, no. There's all sorts depending on the crime. Beatings, splinters under the fingernails, things like that." He dropped the box back at the trunk of the tree. "You don't want to hear any more."

Stolen Children

EVENTUALLY BILLY SPOKE ABOUT HIS YOUTH. During that period, the Australian government had thought that light-skinned and biracial Aboriginal children should be raised in white households. He and many other children had been forcibly removed from their families, split apart from siblings, and raised in foster care.

When they had been old enough to ask about their biological families, the government had withheld the information that would have allowed them to reconnect. Eventually pressure from the worldwide community ended the practice in 1970, although children continued to be removed for several years.

After a life spent between two worlds, Billy had traced his family back to the Alice. His brothers and mother had already regrouped but he rejoined his family just two weeks after his father had died.

After Billy finished speaking, the croak of a single cockatoo was the only sound. His intensely personal story was a damning condemnation of a government that had attempted a form of genocide. I had fled an America I had found increasingly intolerant to find an enduring parallel to the racial hatred embodied in slavery.

As I returned to the car, the blooms of the Stuart's desert pea caught my eye. Blood didn't have to be shed for a family to be murdered.

Silence

SIMPLICITY SOOTHED ALL ANXIETY from my vagabond life. Although I slumbered on different soil almost every evening, my eyes no longer fell upon scenery. The arid sweep from horizon to horizon was my home, the wind a loving friend that stroked my face while bats swung overhead.

My attention shifted to the basics: water for day and warmth for night. In the light the pure rain ran like cool satisfaction over my tongue, and in the dark the heat of sunbeams captured by spinifex and mallee bathed my skin. As I melded with the land, the flow of time loosened. The myriad details so common to daily living whirled away.

My only deliberate thoughts were of when and where to restock the supplies and which patch of earth would prove the most comfortable. Otherwise I absorbed the moods and features of the open desert, the pools of thin grey shade. My life was becoming more connected, groping back through a hundred years of industrialization and mechanized living to some fundamental truth.

Back home, I had been like a bird with clipped wings, capable of parodying flight just well enough to survive. In the extended solitude of the Outback, my feathers began to grow. There was the tang of wood smoke my belly recognized as a precursor to meals, the satisfaction of a filling meal, the gnaw of hunger when supplies ran low.

In the evening, after the dingoes and wombats and bats had paid their respects, came silence. The desert's winter nights shed no sound other than that of my own movement. When the fire died, my ears rang with the quiet.

Killer Caterpillars

THE DAILY SEARCH FOR FIREWOOD took quite a bit of time in the heavily traveled areas. Some trees shed their limbs during drought to conserve moisture and nutrients, and they provided a boon other travelers bypassed. When I broke off the dry lower branches of one tree and dragged the bundle back to camp, the sticks scratched my forearm.

Soon the wound itched and burned. By morning the scratch had blistered, and the surrounding flesh was swollen and angry. I assumed I was having an allergic reaction and headed for the nearest hospital two hundred clicks to the north. Since both my doctor and my dentist had warned me about the unknown evils of socialized medicine, I simply stayed near emergency care in case the arm dropped off unexpectedly.

Five weeks would pass before the welt healed. When I showed the fading injury to a park ranger, I discovered that I had been attacked by a caterpillar. Also known as the spitfire, the baghouse moth caterpillar fed on acacia trees. When food ran out, the colony marched single-file over the desert sands to another acacia.

Its only defense was its spit, a caustic juice that had singed my skin. My efforts to stay safe around venomous snakes and poisonous spiders and toxic plants had been felled by a fuzzy creature less than two inches long.

Bush Tucker

TO FILL THE TIME while I waited to expire from the caterpillar attack, I booked a tour in Tenant Creek. The jaunt would take a group of tourists into the desert to hunt for and sample wild foods.

Three Aboriginal women and a choleric guide drove the 4WD bus down a track nearly obscured by scrub. The guide attempted to stay on the rough track while watching the oldest Aboriginal woman seated directly behind her.

"Here?" the driver frequently asked. "How about here?"

The elder's face remained still as she studied the terrain. A heavy sigh issued from the driver's seat as the guide cast an impatient look into the rearview mirror. Her tone grew more frustrated as the bus penetrated deeper into the scrub.

Eventually the elder raised one hand. The bus dipped wildly as the driver stomped on the brakes. The dozen tourists were each handed a long crowbar and were told to spread out. We were on the trail of the witchetty grub, that colossal, creeping mass of protein.

Witchetty grubs were found, not surprisingly, wherever the witchetty bush grew. This relatively nondescript shrub grew low to the ground and produced waxy seed pods that resembled skinny green beans. The grubs lived in a hollow carved inside the stem; an opening a few inches above the ground was used to push waste out of the chamber. The brownish spoor indicated that a succulent morsel hid within.

"Does it hurt the plant living inside the trunk like that?" asked one traveler.

"Nah," the elder said with a breathy laugh. "Witchetty no kill bush. People do, when get witchetty."

The chase yielded a handful of titanic worms that the driver held out for all to see. Although they weren't difficult to carry, this was only the first of several types of bush tucker we would gather that morning. I pointed to the small canvas tote slung over my shoulder and offered to carry the grubs.

"Certainly not," the driver snapped. "These are for everyone, not just you."

Grub stealing must have been rampant among her other tour groups. I shook off her rudeness and followed the others back to the bus. By the time we arrived, the three Aboriginal women had stripped leaves from a soap tree. Rubbing the leaves and pods vigorously with water, we worked up a lather and cleaned our hands.

"Where did the leaves come from?" I asked.

"I already told you," the driver growled. "They're from the soap tree."

"I understand that," I said slowly. "Is there another name for the tree? If not, could you point it out, *please?*"

"Over there."

She flung her hand toward the sky and stomped onto the bus. Evidently she was too embarrassed to admit that she didn't know.

Witchetties

THE NEXT TRACK followed by the 4WD bus faded rapidly. The branches of stunted trees screeched against the vehicle, and many bushes were crushed beneath the tires. Eventually the elder again raised her hand. We were shown how to dig bush potatoes, a tuber produced by a shrub with wide, round leaves.

The Aboriginal women circled in wide arcs. A slight ripple or crack in the earth would indicate where the shrub's roots had swollen enough to produce an edible hunk. Once the women found a likely prospect, they sat on the ground and chipped away with the crowbars. The younger two occasionally aborted their efforts but the eldest was relentless, knowing with an unspoken confidence that food lay beneath. She was never wrong.

When the youngest woman drifted off, I tagged along. She moved into a patch of bush tomatoes, gangly shrubs with hairy leaves. Earlier in the season the plants had produced a purple bloom with a yellow center. The ripe fruit was gold and about the size of a medium egg. She plucked only the ones that were ripe enough to eat and indicated that I should do the same.

The plants guarded their bounty with four tough fingers studded with thorns. When I gingerly gripped a ripe tomato, it popped easily into my palm. The young woman split the skin with her thumbnail to reveal an interior crammed with large black seeds. She cleared the seeds and then scraped away the innermost layer of pulp.

"Not kill," she said as she shook the pulp from her fingers. "But taste, *pfft,* bad."

She tore off a morsel of the remaining flesh and chewed it slowly. The raw tomato tasted like honeydew melon without any cloying sweetness. We finished the fruit in silence as the wind ruffled our hair and the sun shifted along its arc.

The final stop took us to a clapboard cabin that served as an evening gathering place for local clans. The driver called for the men to fetch some firewood. I was always eager for a tramp through the bush, especially one that would put a little distance between me and a cranky tour guide, and returned with an armload of wood. Unfortunately this only increased the driver's ire.

"Do you think we'll be here all week?" she shouted at me.

The men who had retrieved about the same amount of wood apparently thought this was a private matter and turned away. It was a relief to know that the guide treated all women, not just the Aboriginal ones, with contempt. She might have been an ass but she was an equal-opportunity ass.

A roaring fire—which of course consumed a great deal of the wood the men and I had gathered—heated two huge billies. One supplied water for tea while the other could be used for instant coffee. The embers were raked smooth and the food was dumped unceremoniously on top. Including the grubs. I turned away too slowly and saw them twist atop the coals.

Within minutes the tea was ready, the bush tucker was passed around on pieces of bark, and jam rolls satisfied timid palates. The potato was bland with a hint of nuttiness. The roasted tomatoes had a flavor all their own, a pleasant cross between stewed green tomatoes and melon.

The witchetties were the big surprise. After picking off the worst of the burned bits, I discovered that the cooked grubs tasted exactly like hard-fried eggs. I don't happen to care for fried eggs and the flavor was strong but I ate two just to be certain of my impression.

Because the group had foraged so successfully and eaten so little, a number of potatoes and tomatoes were left over. They hadn't been cooked and so were offered to the tourists to consume later. Only I and one other traveler volunteered to take the remainders. Everyone else seemed pleased to have experimented but uninterested in further experiences with wild tucker.

I asked the youngest Aboriginal woman if she wanted the food. "After all," I said, "you did all the work."

A smile peeked through the hair billowing around her face. She waved at the vast scrub.

"We get this any day," she said. "Like other food, food from the store, better. We eat this only when broke."

Waiting

TURNING EAST ALONG THE BARKLY HIGHWAY, I careened across 500 kilometers and pulled over only when exhausted. After departing the Alice to continue north, the wind had blown for hours every night. The flapping of the tent had kept me awake as dust had sifted through every seam. I hoped to abandon the air spirits by leaving the Northern Territory for Queensland.

The Barkly Plains spread to the horizons, a vast savanna grasslands dotted with trees. An hour spent scrounging for firewood turned up only a bare handful of kindling. I had stocked up a few days earlier and used some of the extra wood strapped onto the roof rack. If the shortage continued, I would have to develop a taste for cold dinners again.

I carefully laid the fire by starting with dried grass twisted together into thin logs. These were covered by twigs leaned together like teepee poles. As the flame grew, I would create teepees of larger sticks until enough embers formed to lay wood on top. A woman carrying a wheel rim and a sheet of tin interrupted my task.

"If you build the fire in the rim," she said, "and shelter the flame with the tin, the fire will burn better. And the rim holds heat well."

I filled the rim with the stones gathered for the fire ring as the woman settled in for a chat. She and her husband Dennis had been stranded there for almost two weeks after their Volkswagen Kombi had broken down.

"Burned valves and a blown gasket," she sighed. "Dennis hitched a ride with a truckie to call the road service but the closest garage is in

Mt. Isa. The auto club wants fourteen hundred dollars to tow the van. That's more than the bloody thing's worth!"

Rather than be robbed, Dennis had decided to fix the motor himself. He had bought the tools he needed and ordered parts before hitching back out. Then they had started the long, lonely job of waiting for the shipment to arrive, waiting for another ride into town, and waiting for a ride back to the van.

"We're fortunate to have broken down near fresh water," she said. "Still, we're going a bit stir crazy what with the wind and no fresh food. Dennis tracked roos hoping to lay a trap along a game trail but neither of us has actually seen any animals since we broke down."

I gave them a few boxes of soup mix, some of the canned mango that was my usual breakfast, and potatoes but didn't have any fresh vegetables or fruits. She was grateful for all of it but particularly for the boxed items because of their flavor packets. At that point, anything different was a welcome addition to their stores.

She immediately retreated to the van with her gifts. Considering their situation, I knew that an invitation to dinner would not be forthcoming. I settled back into my routine, looking forward to the morning when I could travel far enough to escape the wind.

Man Alone

AS DUSK CREPT OVER THE PLAINS, an older man stopped by my camp. He told me he was traveling alone and invited me to eat with him in his trailer. I hadn't started cooking the potatoes that were my usual dinner yet, and the need to preserve firewood made the prospect attractive.

When I accepted, he asked me to bring the kerosene lantern. His equipment was limited to a single large propane tank. With only one hookup, he couldn't run the stove and the lights at the same time. I told him I would top off the lantern and be right over. Soon I rapped on his door.

"Come in, come in!" he cried. "I'm so pleased to have company."

George acted as delighted as if I was a beloved neighbor who had stopped in unannounced. For that night, I was.

His gestures were quick and a little jerky, as if his long limbs were not to be trusted in the cramped space. He stooped beneath the low ceiling while boiling half a dozen eggs. By the time the tea had been poured, he'd laid the table with bread, butter, and two plates. Only when he sat did he straighten fully, finally confident that he had enough room in which to relax.

The tableware included two egg cups. I had never seen them used before and watched as he balanced one of the eggs in the graceful bowl. He was surprised at my lack of experience and said, not unkindly, "Must be an American thing."

Talk of our countries led to talk of our lives. George had grown up in Poland just before World War II, a time of chaotic politics and corruption. Eventually he had decided to flee and had boarded a train in the middle of the night with only the few possessions he could carry.

"A dramatic and pathetic display." He tilted his head. "But my life seemed horrid. My friends and I talked about leaving for a long time. We all wanted something better. But when the time came to pack our bags, I was the only one who went."

He shook his head. "My family, oh, how they cried, and my father, how he yelled. 'Foolish boy,' he said, 'You can't run,' he said, 'Where will you go?'

"I never saw them again. My friends, family, all the ones who stayed behind, they all died in concentration camps."

The silence was filled only by the steady hiss of the gas lantern. After a time, he told me about the life he'd built for himself in Australia. His marriage had lasted decades and ended only when he had become a widower.

"She passed away, let's see, two years ago now, nothing unexpected or painful. We'd planned to travel the country with friends and took a few short trips once I had retired. But we never made the big one together."

He meant the big tour, months spent driving around the country and camping wherever the land looked welcoming.

"Now I'm living the dream," he said. "I go all around, see the country up close, always watching. My friends were enthusiastic enough until time came to leave. They backed out at the last minute. They've nothing to do! They're retired, sitting around at home complaining about being bored and yet were afraid to come."

Again George walked alone. The sadness he felt was natural and formed a soft presence in the dim trailer.

"You have to do what's best for you," I said. "My friends were excited about my trip. They told me about their dreams to travel or to find new careers."

"But they wouldn't dare," he said.

"They had so many excuses. Jobs, family, friends...and fear, I suppose."

"Yes, certainly. They are afraid of what is not common." He glanced out through the window before looking back at me. "It is not safe, this road we travel. They are afraid of what they will find. They might find themselves."

Road Crew

AS I APPROACHED CAMOOWEAL, a long section of road was under repair. The crews usually ran a track through the bush to allow cars to detour around the work but the rains had reduced the trail to a muddy bog. As the muck grew deeper, the steering wheel turned sluggish. Driving through the bog was like driving through snow except that the steering was heavy instead of light.

Using my winter driving skills, I let Chugger slosh along without touching the gas pedal. Until a bus loomed in the side mirror. The machine drew ever closer and clearly needed more speed to keep from sinking. There wasn't enough room for it to pass, so I pushed the car to 30 kph. Anything faster destroyed the tiny bit of steering control.

When I spotted a Kombi mired on one side of the track, I slowed. Chugger had been bogged on a dirt track I'd taken near Uluru, and the last driver to pass by that day had stopped to help me dig the car out. I thought to pay it forward by helping these strangers but a sharp blast of the coach's horn encouraged me to keep moving.

Even though I pushed the car, the bus repeatedly caught up and pressed from behind. Whenever the mud thinned a bit, I poured on more speed. But there were times when Chugger simply couldn't maintain traction and I was forced to slow down.

As the bus and I played this sloppy game of chase, an obstacle loomed in the road. One of the work crew had parked a truck in the middle of the track. Standing beside it were two blokes casually sipping away at steaming cups of tea. My only option was to sling the car into a half skid through the deeper muck on the right side.

Momentum kept Chugger moving along the curve and the car regained the center. Moments later another construction vehicle squelched toward me on what passed for the shoulder. The driver leaned out the window waving and shouting. Something worse lay ahead, and he clearly didn't want any vehicles to encounter that something.

By that point, the track had become a real mire. There would be no stopping for anyone who didn't want to stick around for a few days until the mud dried. That bus and I continued running full out, hell-bent for pavement. A few grinding, slurping minutes later, another construction vehicle crawled toward us. This driver gesticulated even more wildly. I just waved.

"Get along, little doggies!" I whooped.

A road train loomed ahead. The roadbed was raised, and I saw a line of vehicles sitting behind the tractor trailer. I was going to make it!

But wait. What was that vast, rumpled thing strewn across the track? It was a churned up pit of mud. Mounds of muck corralled lakes of rainwater. Chunks of goo had been sprayed everywhere by other vehicles, and there was no telling how deep the pool at the middle was.

I had to stop. No, that bus would slide right into me. Go!

I needed momentum, a ton of momentum. I goosed the gas as much as I dared and felt the front wheels glide atop the mud. Faster! I needed more speed to sling the car through to the road. Faster now as the rear of the car slipped to one side. I let off the gas for an instant and goosed it again.

Chugger slewed sideways just as it hit the bog. Water splashed the windshield and left the view a brown fog. Turning into the skid, I took both feet off the pedals. The car bounced and whipped the other direction. I gunned the pedal once when the wheels caught and let off again. Suddenly we were clear!

I powered up the slope and surfaced on the bitumen. The walleyed truck drivers gawped at me as the car squeezed past. Pounding the steering wheel, I shouted, "Viva Australia! Yee-ha!"

I don't know how long the other travelers were stuck there but Chugger had conquered another Outback challenge.

White Ants

THE COACH ALSO EMERGED from the mud but fell behind as I skittered along the remaining few miles to Camooweal. Chugger needed petrol, so I decided to fill up and then treat myself to a well-earned coffee break. As I pumped gas, the bus rumbled to a halt. The door swooshed open and the driver trotted over.

"I didn't mean to chase you," he said, "but stopping would have gotten us stuck. And after the first bit I couldn't have stopped anyway. If you had slowed, I'd have run right over you."

I told him it was all right, that it had been a matter of survival. As he disappeared into the roadhouse, passengers straggled over in clumps of two or three. Suddenly I was awash in excitement and noise.

"Good driving!" shouted one passenger inches from in my ear.

He offered me a hearty smile and a heartier whack on the shoulder. One man who had headed directly for the café paused at the door. He turned to peer at me before tapping his wife on the shoulder.

"It's a sheila!" he said. "Didn't know a sheila could drive like that!"

"She's a Yank," someone called, as if that would explain why a woman could possess such exceptional vehicular skills.

Another fellow pushed his cane into the ground with both hands. "We were rooting for you," he said. "Did you see us leaning out the windows?"

"Um, no," I said. "I was focused on getting out of there."

"We were waving our hats and shouting like we were as crazy as white ants!"

"You're the most entertaining thing I've seen on this bloody tour," another person said. "Broke the monotony, you did."

Yet another fellow pushed around the car and grabbed my free hand to shake it vigorously.

"I'd like to thank you," he said, "for being the most exciting part of the trip so far!"

On that tour, at least, the customers got their money's worth.

Red Glow

A PATCHWORK OF ASPHALT wound toward the next town. The paved lanes expanded and contracted from one to two and back again like the scribbles left by a snake. At Mount Isa's Aboriginal cultural center, a teenager played a tune on his didgeridoo and then demonstrated how the objects on display were used.

A gunyah, a domed hut made of branches and scrub, had been built in one corner. The roof had been tightly thatched to shed rain. Any nearby trees would have been cut back to prevent falling branches from destroying the gunyahs. A small trough dug into the surrounding earth would have channeled runoff away from the interior.

At the rear of the building, a bare concrete area, the boy offered to show me how to start a fire. He plucked sand from a crack in the floor, dropped a few grains into a small hole in a stick, and added wisps of grass. Steadying the branch between his bare feet, he spun the end of another stick rapidly in the bowl.

After several attempts, a thin tendril of smoke rewarded his efforts. The boy demonstrated how the ember would be tipped onto a pile of dried grass and gently blown into life. He grinned sheepishly and apologized for having taken so long; his uncle, he said, could start a fire on the second or third try.

"If I practice enough," he said with a spark like diamonds bright in his eyes, "soon I will be like him."

It is often said that the youths are our hope for a shining future. Perhaps this boy, already so proud of his tradition, carried ancient embers in his heart so that Australia's red glow would never fade.

Lakeview

THE LAKEVIEW STATION AT BALFE'S CREEK offered a taste of life on an Aussie ranch. A drought had plagued the cattle ranches for so long that many places had opened their yards and porches to travelers. If a tourist could get there on their own, they were welcome to stay for a very affordable nightly fee. Some ranches offered meals for a bit extra.

The homestead at Lakeview had a screened rear porch that served as the main entrance. A dilapidated truck with yawing holes rusted through the fenders stood guard. The tiny bit of grass spread out before the porch had been encircled with barbed wire to prevent horses and cattle from destroying the lawn.

A corral behind the house detained nervous weaners, calves that had been removed from their mothers a bit early. If left with the cows, the calves would have exhausted and killed their mothers with their demands for milk. Although the drive ended at that point, I couldn't find a gate. When I attempted to squeeze between the barbed wire, I wound up on my butt.

As I dusted off my already dusty shorts, an older woman wearing a gauzy dress stepped out of the ranch house. Bea nodded when I mentioned the flier advertising ranch stays. Her grey pageboy swiveled as she scanning the horizon, perhaps looking for the son who would soon return to the house. She led me onto the screened porch where we enjoyed a cup of tea and spun away the afternoon.

"The family's gathering for a barbie tonight," she said. "You're more than welcome as my guest. Just pull your car through the paddock and park near the lawn. I think the bulls are in the west paddock, so you'll be fine."

I was glad to hear that I wouldn't have to deal with any stray bulls. During a camping trip in Oklahoma, a friend and I had evacuated our campsite due to the very aggressive growls of an animal that had come sniffing after our steak dinner. Hours later, we crept back to the site to see if it was safe to return.

The fire had burned down and the growling beast was still around...and was still aggressively vocalizing its desire to be left alone. I'd managed to snag our sleeping bags from the tent before it had come crashing back through the trees, so we retreated again and slept in the middle of the path.

A mere hour after falling asleep, I was awoken by a snuffing blow. The herd of buffalo moseying along the track would certainly be as domineering as the snarling beastie. I shook my friend awake, whispered urgently for her to follow, and scrambled under a concrete picnic table.

When the herd made it clear that they liked this patch of grass for grazing, thank you very much, we'd squirmed into our bags and slept sandwiched between the benches and the pillar holding up the table.

Camping in an empty pasture was a fine idea. Except that the pasture wouldn't be entirely bull-free.

"The one we're fixing to slaughter is in there," Bea said. "But he's lame, so I reckon he won't do you no harm."

Cattle ranchers tended to run Brangus, a hearty breed that crossed Angus with the tough Brahman. Although the temperament of domesticated breeds was somewhat less touchy than the wild water buffalo in Australia's northern regions, any animal that size deserved respect. I decided to pitch my tent as close to a gate or fence as possible.

"You can use the toilet in the house anytime," Bea said. "Just be sure to keep the gate to the yard shut so the pony don't get out. We keep a Shetland near the house here so it can feed on some good grass."

Ponies were much better company than buffalo and bulls, I decided.

"Phew!" Bea cried. "What's that stink?"

She opened the screen door to investigate. A whiff of something dead wafted across the porch as a Labrador mix looked up from its meal. Apparently it had found something delectable and carried it home to enjoy in peace. Bea quickly put an end to its meal.

"Ugh, you smell worse than that meat!" she said.

She grabbed something that might have been a hoof and dragged the haunch toward the drive.

"The dog might try to get in your tent to sleep with you," she called over her shoulder. "He's harmless, so don't be afraid."

Fear certainly wasn't what prevented me from giving the pungent dog a scratch behind the ears. Bea heaved the leg into the drive and then returned to the porch. The dog stared indignantly at her retreating figure before trotting over to retrieve the snack. After carrying it back to the grass, it flopped down with a happy sigh and resumed gnawing.

With so many four-legged visitors likely to drop by, it would be an interesting stay.

Steaks and Snakes

LATE THAT AFTERNOON, a boisterous crowd of family and neighbors appeared at the Lakeview homestead. We hauled tables and chairs onto the lawn to prepare for the barbie.

I offered to fire up the grill, a chore made difficult by the lack of kindling. I had created what I considered to be a fairly large blaze when Dob, a leather-faced, wrinkle-eyed, gruff-and-grumble Aussie, clomped up.

"Where's the fire?" he bellowed. "You call that a fire? I'll show you a fire!"

He chucked log after log onto the flames until smoke billowed up in thick clouds. For the next ten minutes, he leaned into the smoke and stoked with his hat. The entire time, his lips went like the clappers. Most of his tirade was aimed at Yanks and their ignorance about Australian culture.

"I know what you Yanks say about us Aussies," he brayed, seemingly unfazed by the smog he was inhaling. "Put another shrimp on the barbie, you say. If I have enough bloody money for a bucket of prawns I'd be a silly wanker to ruin them on the barbie! Wouldn't I?"

He aimed the question at one of Bea's sons.

"Yeah, I reckon." Kevin grinned at me.

"All you Yanks think we're Crocodile Dundee out here, wrestling crocodiles and running around in the bush!"

Between the explosive rounds of teasing, several people wandered over to eye the large stack of steaks thawing on the table. And when I say stack, I mean a mound that was as high as my arm was long.

The crowd prodded different pieces to measure the trim with fingertips and eyes. Then they rejoined the group at the grill and proclaimed, "There's nothing better than a nice piece of fat."

Which made me realize why Australian grills were topped with flat griddles rather than open grates. If an actual chunk of lard was desirable then retaining as much grease as possible must also have been important. And, it seemed, the more meat the better. Steak was almost always accompanied by sausages, wryly called snakes.

This fleshy repast was relished with the second important Aussie food group, salt. The sizzling barbie was layered with salt, wiped clean, and blanketed with a fresh coat of white crystals. The meat was also liberally sprinkled as it cooked, the frequency of which occurred in direct proportion to the number of beers consumed by the cook.

Although I was overwhelmed by new faces and names, the gaggle of kids zooming around on big wheels, and the pack of Chihuahuas and whippets underfoot, I gorged on steak and sausage. Hamburgers and chicken pasta were also on offer but I passed those over; there just wasn't enough room in my stomach. A few token vegetables, neglected and forlorn, shriveled as the hours progressed.

With his smoky hat firmly clamped atop his head, Dob waved a beer in my direction. I turned him down yet again. I wasn't much of a drinker and beer wasn't high on my list of favorites, so I sipped a rum and coke.

"Well, no wonder you can't build a fire!" Dob roared. "Anyone who drinks that slow must be a lazy worker!"

Assistant Rancher

EARLY THE NEXT MORNING, I fixed my breakfast and joined Bea on the porch for tea. Her son Kevin popped in to run down the list of chores with her. Then he turned to me.

"You want to come along?" he asked.

"All tours of the property are complimentary," Bea said.

"I'd love to go," I said. "If I can lend a hand anywhere, I'd be glad to help out."

Kevin grinned because, I though, he was happy to have such an eager assistant. I would soon discover that he was happiest over having a sidekick to torment with that mischievous Aussie humor.

"Today we're putting out lick for the cattle," he said as we strode to the storage shed. "We do it every other day, less often when there's no drought. It rained a few days ago, so I have to tip out the barrels and load them with fresh lick."

"Ah," I said and nodded. "What's lick?"

"Feed we mix up special depending on what the herd needs." He tugged open the shed door. "Right now we use a lot of urea. It's fine in the lick but when it rains, the urea dissolves into the water. Bloody cows drink that off the top of the feed barrels rather than go a little extra way to the pond. Too much will kill them, so I'll tip the old lick out on the ground."

Kevin hefted a fifty-kilo bag to his shoulder in a way that made it look fairly easy. But I knew the weight would come in at over a hundred pounds and didn't attempt to move any of the sacks.

"What's urea for?" I asked. "It doesn't sound like something you'd want in cattle feed."

"During drought," he said, "the grass is dry and doesn't have much nutrition. So we feed lick to make up for that. But it's expensive and takes time to put out. The urea makes the cows hungry so they'll eat more grass. Eating more than they usually would helps make up for the poor nutrition."

As he continued moving sacks, I asked if there was anything lighter he needed on the truck.

"I'll want three of those."

He waved at a stack of forty-kilo bags. I staggered to the truck twice before deciding that a third was out of the question.

"You could load that."

He pointed to a small bag. I grabbed the twisted neck and started to stand but was caught short by the unexpected weight.

"Careful," he called just then. "It's heavy."

The truck was driven only a few feet to the mixer, a long, barrel-shaped hopper atop a lattice of rickety steel legs. A wide gap cut from the top allowed the feed to be poured into the hopper at any point along its length. Inside, three spiraling bands of steel rotated through the feed to mix everything evenly.

Once the motor chugged into life, Kevin indicated that I should stand on top. I climbed from the truck to my assigned perch. Since there was no grate over the gap, I dug the soles of my boots into the lip of the opening to prevent slips. After dumping about half the feed directly into the center, Kevin handed the bags up to me so I could pour the feed out at either end.

The barrel shuddered with every clank of the engine, and the contraption swayed whenever a full bag hit the edge. I had always been a little leery of heights, so straddling a weak-legged barrel of rusty steel wasn't fun. But I got into the rhythm of the work and soon we were down to the last two bags.

The motor driving the mixing blades must not have been fully up to the task. It hiccupped a few times before suddenly powering up well past its former speed. The banging and coughing set the mixer shaking like a wet dog. My reflexes took over and I leapt down to the truck bed, landing on my feet before whipping around to watch the mixer tip over.

It didn't, and Kevin stared at me for a moment before breaking into a whooping laugh.

"I've never seen anybody move like that before!" he said. "Do all you Yanks move so quick?"

Only those with strong survival instincts.

Tipping at Windmills

AFTER LOADING THE LICK ONTO THE TRUCK, Kevin and I climbed into the cab and careened around the property. The cattle station consisted of thousands of acres leased from the government, a common arrangement in a land too poor to support cattle efficiently.

Kevin told me about his plan to create more pasture. He had sent a petition to the government asking permission to fell trees on another ten thousand acres. If the request was approved, the family would string a heavy chain between two tractors or a tractor and a truck and then drive around ripping trees out of the ground. The felled timber would be burned to prevent a bushfire.

The family made use of all the treasures on the property, and Kevin had loaded a rifle into the cab of the truck for just that reason. When he spotted a mob of kangaroos grazing on a hilltop, he reached for the weapon. Before he could draw a bead on one of the creatures, the mob had hopped away.

"Too bad," I said. "I had a roo steak at a restaurant in Adelaide, and it tastes great. It would have been a nice addition to your next family barbie."

He peered at me as if I might be joking. To him, kangaroos were dogfood. Some ranchers thought it was healthy for the dogs. And of course it was free.

"Used to work on another fellow's station when I was younger," he said. "Part of my job was to shoot five roos every day for the dogs. He had a lot of dogs. Just couldn't stomach it after a while, though, all that waste. But once in a while it's OK. Besides, they eat the grass and the cattle are already hungry."

The cattle industry, with its emphasis on pastures and water holes, had accidentally created explosive population growth among the animals it considered pests. Land that could support one cow could support several kangaroos. The government stepped in to provide roo shooters. They camped on cattle stations and culled animals until the quota for that property was filled.

We settled into a comfortable silence as emus flashed among the trees. Whenever we came to a gate, I hopped out to open the portal so the truck could drive through. Kevin appreciated the assistance because it shaved precious minutes off of the task. The next time I clambered into the cab, I presented another ranching question.

"Ever have a problem with cow tipping?" I asked.

"With what?"

"Cow tipping. You know, where two or three people sneak up on a sleeping cow and sort of body slam it. Knocks them right off their feet. I figured you'd be close enough to town so that drunk teenagers might try it with your stock."

He studied me closely.

"No," he finally said. "Don't know what kind of cows you got in the States but we run Brahman. They're foul-tempered enough to hold their own against a few drunks. What did you call that again?"

"Cow tipping."

He remained quiet as we lurched toward the next trough. Eventually he pointed to a black cylinder. It was an old tractor-trailer tire minus the sidewalls. With one edge buried a few inches in the ground, the tire became a small well.

"For a few hours and the price of a razor," Kevin said, "I have a well where I can't afford to put in a pond. Cheap enough, so long as I don't slice off a finger."

We stopped at his house for smoko, a sort of coffee break with a mini-meal. His wife Tess fed us flapjacks smeared with syrup and butter. While her husband worked the property, she managed the house, their child, and odd ranch chores. After they had lined up the tasks to be completed, we returned to the truck.

Soon we passed another windmill. I had noticed several scattered around the desert during my trip and had assumed that they generated electricity for lonely huts hidden by the distance. But on Lakeview, their placement was puzzling.

"Why are the windmills so far away from the house?" I asked.

"Hey?" Kevin asked.

"The windmills. Why do you have them so far away from the house? Are the electric cables underground?"

He took a long moment to respond. When he did speak, it was with the steady patience of an adult explaining a simple fact to a child.

"Windmills are powered by wind," he said. "That's why they're called windmills."

"No," I said with a laugh. "I know that. But why are they way out here? They're generating electricity, right?"

"The windmills pump water. They pull groundwater up into the cattle ponds."

"Interesting. In America we use windmills to generate electricity."

He knocked his hat down over his eyes and peered at me from under the rim.

"I don't know anything about that," he said. "That something like cow tipping?"

Thirst

THE NEXT DAY I LAZED ABOUT, chatting with Bea's friends and neighbors. After I drained my tea, I went into the kitchen for a glass of water. A liquid as white as diluted milk splashed from the tap. The appearance didn't put me off but the first sip encouraged me to set the beverage on the side table.

As the group continued chattering, I calculated how soon I could sneak back into the kitchen and tip out the foul stuff. Clearly I would have to rely on my own supplies during my visit. After purchasing the car in Sydney, I'd gone to a bar and bought several of the plastic containers used to transport large quantities of alcohol. After a quick rinse, the sturdy receptacles became perfect vessels for long-term camping needs.

Every roadhouse offered a public tap where travelers could resupply their potable water. At key points along the most remote roads...meaning most of Australia's interior highways...the government had constructed large holding tanks that gathered rainwater for the same purpose.

I'd learned early on to refill from the rain tanks whenever possible. The water that flowed from faucets might have been safe to drink but the amount of dissolved solids made it less than palatable. Maybe Aussies drank so much tea to kill the harsh flavors.

Since I had already turned down Bea's offer of tea, I would have to wait to quench my thirst. After a few minutes, during which the swirling goo that I refused to drink continued to swirl, Bea eyed the glass.

"Did you use the main tap," she asked, "or the faucet to the side?"

"The main tap."

"That's bore water," she said, meaning well water. "It's safe enough but if you'd like rainwater then use the other faucet."

I trotted back to the kitchen and gulped down a refreshing cup. After the other visitors left, Bea invited me to go with her to tend the bore pump. We drove deep into the paddock closest to the homestead and parked beside a diesel-powered pump. She rapped the fuel drum to check its level and cranked up the motor.

"Water's pumped from here to the tank beside the house," she said. "Spent near ten thousand dollars drilling wells. Then we found some but the pressure was so low it would've run dry too quick. Right before we ran out of money, we struck good water. We've been lucky."

When the tank looming above the house overflowed, Bea drove out again to shut off the pump. Gravity fed the water into the house where it was used for everything except drinking and cooking.

The dissolved solids were normally harmless for livestock but rendered the supply useless for agriculture. In some places where groundwater bubbled up naturally, the solids deposited during evaporation grew so thick atop the plants that they died from lack of sunlight.

"I saw you drinking the bore water right off," she said, "but I didn't want to say anything. Thought maybe you liked it, you being a Yank and all."

We might eat donuts for breakfast but not even a Yank would drink bore water.

A Killing

THE LAME BULL SHARING THE PADDOCK with my tent was judged to be fat enough for slaughter. Bea's other son Rob used a dirt bike, the modern drover's mount, to cruise through the pasture until he located the animal. Behind the bike, a plume of dust rose like the ostrich feathers that crowned a New Orleans funeral carriage.

The bull was dispatched with a single rifle shot to the head. By the time Kevin and I arrived in a crane, a lake of blood had pooled around its head. The gash along its throat gushed a hot fountain from which the dogs eagerly lapped.

A hook on the end of the crane was run through the shin of one leg. The carcass was winched into the air where it dangled loosely, its joints liquid in death. With every bump during the return trip, the soft muzzle was bruised against the ground. It felt as if we were being chased.

At one end of a concrete slab near the corral stood a sturdy metal frame. The bull's hind legs were spread between the bars, and the hulk was efficiently disemboweled, beheaded and dismembered. Each crack of a knee joint, each juicy spray from the impact of an ax filled the air with timeless sounds.

The silent pirouettes of flashing blades removed every reminder of life. The animal was reduced to its lowest common denominator, haunches and ribs and loins that would provide many meals. The biography of scars and fleas and gut and shit were heaped into a puddle near which the dogs whined. As the quarters were lowered onto a meat sheet, an old linen spread across the bed of a truck, Kevin chased the dogs from the viscera.

"You gonna eat the organs?" I asked.

"Nah. Trash," he replied.

"Then why not let the dogs have it?"

He looked blank for a second. "Dunno."

He skimmed another rock at a dog nibbling the hide. Meat hooks swung as the quarters were stored in the cold room, a modest refrigerated shed that stood beside the homestead. The naked hunks were still twitching as they disappeared behind the frosty door. A pair of cockatoos huddled inside their cage as if expecting the blades to flash for them next.

I returned to the concrete slab to retrieve the camera case. Although pocket-sized cameras were on the market then, I had invested in a photojournalist's rig. Documenting lifestyles was as important to me as capturing the landscape, so recording this ranch chore had seemed natural. As I put everything away, Kevin pointed at the rest of the family with his chin.

"They reckon you're a little weird," he said, "taking pictures of the killing and all. But you're a Yank, so it's OK."

I shrugged off their looks. The same men had swung their children up onto the fence near the butchering slab to ensure that they had a clear view. My dad had done the same when I was younger but he had taken us to the butcher shop to watch a side of beef being dismantled. The ranch chore had been quite a bit gorier, and encouraging the children to watch had seemed strange to me.

But they were Aussies, so it was OK.

Muster

AS THE DAYS PASSED, I recognized that Bea took in visitors more for the company than anything else. Whenever I popped into the house for tea or a snack, she invited me to sit with her at the dinner table or join her on the porch. Those shared moments gave me a closer look at ranching and the hardships the family endured to keep their lifestyle alive.

"Fire claimed the original homestead," she said. "Family's been on the land since the early 70s and it's not always been easy."

Her husband Mel, whom I had glimpsed now and then, shuffled onto the porch. He hovered beside the table, looking from an empty chair to the window as if he had lost something.

"Mel here trained racehorses until his accident," Bea said. "Go on, Mel, sit down. It's all right."

"What kind of horses did you train?" I asked as he gingerly sank into the chair.

"All kinds," Bea replied. "Mel, show her your pictures. You want to see some of the horses he trained? Go on, they're in the living room."

I followed the tall, grey apparition into the house. His skin looked as if his flesh might flake wetly from his bones. His slippers, neither of which ever fully left the ground, rasped against the parquet like sandpaper. As we passed the bedroom where he spent most of his time, the scent of a lingering illness crept through the doorway.

Mel raised one thin arm at a gallery of photos that crowded the walls all the way to the ceiling. The horses were magnificent, and their coats gleamed beneath the rays of faraway days. Although Mel was slow to answer my questions and was clearly frustrated by his inability to express his thoughts, pride shone in his eyes like distant beacons.

Bea overheard us talking and discovered that I used to jump horses in equestrian shows. She arranged for Ben, a teenager from another family living on the station, to escort me on a ride using the ranch's horses.

This was no small endeavor. First Kevin and Ben had to take the dirt bikes out to a different paddock where the horses grazed. After a short time, they drove a group of ponies into a small corral. As the herd milled and wheeled, the men moved through the chaos holding ropes.

They quickly cut two animals from the group, coaxed them into halters, and opened the gate. The free horses cantered away, leaving dust and two prancing ponies behind. After a quick grooming, the hooves were checked and the saddles were cinched tightly. Bea listened to Ben's plans for our trip, nodding when he told her which pastures he would take me through, and we swung atop our mounts.

The Good Life

AT FIFTEEN, BEN HAD NOT yet obtained the odd tan pattern of the older men, a walnut complexion capped by pink where the hat blocked the sun. But he was lanky and moved with the ease of someone used to plenty of physical activity. He was as easygoing with conversation, pointing out natural elements he appreciated before lapsing into a companionable silence.

More than once, a brown ball of feathers exploded from beneath our horses' hooves. The birds were a type of pigeon native to the area, and like most pigeons, they waited until the last moment to flee. The ponies jolted but didn't startle. Ben warned me to be careful nevertheless, and although I gave the mare her head, I stayed alert.

We moved along at a sedate walk. Several times, though, my mount simply took off. I reined Beauty in and allowed Ben to catch up.

"Seems like she's triggered by the cows," I said. "That's weird. Why does she go after them like that?"

"We normally only ride to muster cattle," Ben said. "She thinks we're gonna chase some cows around."

"Well, she seems pretty eager. Like it's a game."

"Maybe."

We fell back into enjoying the peace. Whenever we passed near a tree, Ben searched the tall trunks for hollow spaces. If he found one, he would watch for bees, the tiny native species that lacked a stinger. They created nests using beeswax and resin gathered from trees. Inside lay the treasure called sugarbag honey. If Ben found a nest, he would return to the house for a container and harvest the sugarbag.

"We come out here a lot to catch pigs," he said. "We pen the wild ones near the house and fatten 'em up. Chasing them is wild, though. We usually do that on dirt bikes. Run it until it's exhausted."

"Sounds noisy," I said.

"Sometimes they hide under a bush having a rest." He shook his head. "I hate that the most because I'm always the one who's gotta go in after them. Usually they run out the other side but if they decide to charge instead, it can be scary."

The pigs were the descendants of domestic hogs released by Captain Cook when he first landed on Australia's shores. Over time they had become larger and more aggressive. At 150 pounds, a single bore was more than capable of goring a human. Ben must have been especially brave to duck through shrubs where the grunters hid. But those adventures were far different than the ones he longed to experience.

"Been to Townsville yet?" he asked.

"I'm headed there next."

"When I graduate," he said, "I reckon I'll spend some time there. I've been to Charter's Towers, which is only twenty clicks from here, but it's not very big. Townsville's got more people and it'll be different."

"It'll be different, all right," I said. "I reckon I'd stay right here."

"Why?"

"Seems like the good life to me. Living with the land, being outside every day, working with animals...pretty perfect."

Ben mulled for a moment as the creak of our saddles filled the silence.

"Most people who come through tell me that," he said. "They say how lucky I am. I reckon I wouldn't like working inside all the time in an office but I want to see what the city is like. My sister lives there and talks about going out at night to discos and stuff, and all the lights and music."

He looked up to consider the sky and then scanned the pasture.

"Charter's Towers don't have anything like that," he said. "Around here if you want something to do at night, you gotta go to town for movies. Fellow down the road does that once a month, just rents a box of movies to last awhile 'cause he's bored. Can you imagine renting a box of videos? Think of the fees!"

This quiet young man would explore the tales of glitter and pomp, of pollution and crime, and would find more of himself along the way. Even though Ben was drawn by the city and I was repelled, he and I walked the same path. Every step brought us closer to our own souls, a journey that would never end.

Shag on a Rock

AFTER A SHORT TIME IN TOWNSVILLE, I headed north. The subtropical jungles came right up to the coast and would be the place where I would book a few tours. An adventure in a sea kayak was on that list.

Peter, a bronze fellow built like a freight train, churned the beach sand as we moved toward the water. I was his only customer that day, so we pulled a two-person craft through the surf.

"Pity you already paid," he mused. "I would've taken you out for the price of lunch. I just want my customers to have a great time. What else you planning to do here?"

"I bought a ticket for the Hook Island ferry," I said. "The agent kept pressuring me to buy a cruise. She kept saying there wasn't anything on Hook Island. To me, that was the whole point."

"Yeah, people are like that. They want a destination, a name, something to gawk at. They can't just enjoy this."

He swept his hand at the shoreline where the sunlight poured a quicksilver luster atop the waves. Eventually we rounded a point where we were sheltered from the headwind.

"Been through the rain forest yet?" Peter asked.

I told him I had but that the experience had been ruined by the tour guide. The group had stopped in a clearing to make tea and nibble on jam cakes. Not long after we had settled in, a scrub turkey had come out of the woods to investigate.

A woman who tried to chase it away had gotten a peck on the ankle. After that, the tour guide had thrown balls of tinfoil to drive it off. Then he'd bragged about the time he'd kicked the bird so hard it hadn't returned for a few days.

"I know that guy," Peter said. "He and his dad bought the company a year ago. The son knows as much about the rain forest as I know about neurosurgery. Did you report him?"

"I didn't know where to go. I thought I'd write the Queensland Tourist Board."

"He's gotta respect what we've got. If not for the environment then for the tourism that feeds his bloody yap." With an unconscious flex of his muscles, Peter muttered, "I'll have a talk with that fellah. I'll take care of it."

In the quiet filled only by wind and waves, I was free to glory in the sights. And Peter's broad back with all those muscles bunched beneath his nut-brown skin was quite a sight. I normally didn't go for body-builder types but his sense of humor meshed well with mine, the sun was shining, the salt air invigorated my libido, and his teeth shone white, white, white against his dark face.

Eventually I tore my eyes from all that loveliness and gazed at the water, a shimmering green I had only ever seen in pictures of the Caribbean. The water drifted so clear beneath us the rocks were visible. Stands of mangroves mobbed the shore like women groping for crustaceans. Perched on the tips of exposed rocks, black-and-white cormorants known as shags kept vigil. Sea turtles drifted on the surface like bumpy dinner plates.

Although we no longer had to talk over the wind, most of our journey was quiet. We both seemed to prefer it that way.

Cat for Dinner

PETER AND I BEACHED in a cove where we could eat lunch. We roosted with our toes in the sand long after the sandwiches were gone to chat about our lives.

For most of the year, Peter lived in a treehouse in an unregulated portion of the rainforest. The structure consisted of a platform with a single wall. The other sides and the roof were made of netting to keep out the mosquitoes. When the wet season arrived, he stayed at a friend's house.

"A few years back," he said, "my girlfriend moved into the treehouse with her two cats. I don't like cats, they eat too many of the native animals. The feral ones are shot on sight in most parts of Australia because they've impacted some of the endangered animals."

His attitude about cats meant that when a carpet python snagged one for dinner, he wasn't inclined to interfere. Besides, by the time his girlfriend saw what had happened, the pet was likely dead. The tail was the only part visible in the mass of the snake's coils.

"But she kept on bloody screaming for me to do something," Peter said with a sigh. "So my friend and I went after it with a shovel and crowbar. Had the hardest time finding the snake's head. We got the cat back, and damned if it didn't start breathing a few minutes later. It had a few broken ribs but otherwise was fine. Just covered in snake spit is all."

He laughed at the memory and then gave me a wry smile.

"My girlfriend came back just long enough to pack her bags. She was pissed off because I had asked, 'What's the big deal? You have another cat.' She didn't much care for that."

Our return to Airlie Beach was choppy and the currents were against us. I trailed a hand line in hopes of catching a barramundi, a popular entree, but the barra sulked beneath the heaving depths. We spotted a sea snake, a wiggly, intuitive line that drew and erased itself on the watery blackboard.

Peter estimated that we had cruised over forty kilometers. Although he had done most of the work, my arms felt dead. I wearily regarded the beach, which had stretched longer because the tide had receded. The kayak had to be hauled back up the sand, over a low fence, and into a storage shed. And there didn't appear to be any brawny fellows at whom I could bat my eyes and con into carrying my section.

Peter wasn't much help. Every time I hoisted the front end, I tottered only a few steps before he cracked a joke or repeated one of the ribald comments we had swapped that day, which forced me to lower the boat to the sand until the giggling passed.

Only later did I consider that each time I bent over to take up or discard my burden, Peter had enjoyed an enticing view of my butt.

Stinging Nasties

AFTER A LONG DAY OF SIGHTSEEING, I realized that my exhaustion was due to a fever. Chugger's seat never felt cozier as I shut the door against a chilly drizzle. I floated back to the caravan park wanting nothing more than a long snuggle in my swag.

But on this day there were battles to be fought. A squadron of green ants, knocked from their tree by the rain, stood guard on the crossbeams of the tent. They were a type of weaver ant that joined leaves together to create a home, and they packed a nasty sting. I had already experienced their venom once. I had no desire to experience that pain a second time.

I rattled the tent, *my* tent, my *home,* to shake off the invaders. The barbarians clung stubbornly to the plastic, intent upon colonizing this lovely perch. Little pity lay in my heart for their needs, so I broke out the repellant. They lapped up the shower of chemicals as if it was a gentle, refreshing rain. They raised their glowing butts and spread their pincers wide. This was the fulfillment of the green-ant dream: to fight, to bite, even to die.

There was no choice but to squash them one by one. They remained immobile, wound like springs, waiting for the stick to waver close enough for them to latch on. Eventually I drove them away and was able to sleep unmolested.

After resting for a few days, I decided that Australia was a place where I could live. Spending so much time deep in nature's belly had loosened the fetters that held me. The cycles of day and night, light and dark, feast and lean had brought me a deep peace.

Every day I saw something for the first time in my life. This land and these people had opened my heart to the possibilities inherent in every minute. The dust that beat in my blood was far from desolate, and I wanted never to leave my heartland.

Townsville was large enough to host an immigration office, so I returned to the city to explore my options.

"Could you tell me how I would go about immigrating into this country?" I asked the clerk.

"You can't," she said flatly.

I waited but no further explanation was offered. Was I too short? Too tall? Did they not admit bleached blonds?

"Well, why not?" I asked.

"You just can't. It's not allowed."

She barely looked at me. She stood behind a counter in an office that was empty of other workers and other customers. Nothing lay on the counter before her. When I had stepped inside, she hadn't glanced over. She had simply continued staring at the wall with a hundred-mile gaze.

Perhaps that attitude had been cultivated to drive off the pesky people she might otherwise have been expected to help. But I was determined to find out whatever I could about immigration procedures. I was also not one to back down from a fight.

"Is there a particular reason?" I finally asked.

Sighing deeply, she gathered herself for yet another lecture to yet another foreigner who was too ignorant to understand the complex rules and regulations that kept her so terribly busy.

"You can't apply while you are in the country," she said. "You must physically leave the country before you can apply."

Her stare finally shifted to me where it drilled a hole neatly into my forehead so that her words might sink in quickly. The policy made sense. Anyone who was denied entry while in the country could easily disappear into the bush or one of the large cities.

"All right then," I said. "Once I leave the country, how do I apply?"

Her expression warned me that her blood pressure was rocketing from high to explosive.

"I just told you," she growled, "you can't apply now."

My own blood pressure scooted up a notch. A calm facade and excruciating civility controlled my emotions.

"I understand that, ma'am. I would like to know about the application procedure after I leave the country. What sorts of forms should I fill out? Will I have to pass any tests? Are there financial or other requirements?"

"Yes," she spat, and then said nothing more.

I thought my eyes would pop out of their sockets. My next question was delivered in a voice that was barely above a whisper.

"Yes, what, ma'am?"

"Yes, there will be forms and yes, you will have to take the points test."

"I see. And what sort of test is the points test?"

"It's the points test. It rates your eligibility to enter the country in points."

"Mm-hmm. What types of questions might be on this test?"

"*Points* questions," she fumed. "Questions to see whether you are eligible to emigrate."

Her frizzy hair began to tremble. I realized I was speaking to no less an abomination than Medusa, only instead of using her steely scowl to turn me to stone she would petrify me with my own rage. I tried one last question.

"Do you have a sample of this test that I might see?"

"I told you, you can't apply."

"Yes, ma'am."

"You're not going to get in."

"I understand that, ma'am."

"I won't take your application."

"Of course not, ma'am."

The seconds ticked along, ponderous and apocalyptic, until her iron gaze failed. She slapped one palm on the counter and shuffled several inches to her right. Summoning her remaining energy, she lifted a few pamphlets from a shelf and shoved them toward me.

"Thank you and have a *lovely* day," I said.

Paradise

MURRAY FALLS WAS PROTECTED by the boundaries of Girramay National Park. There the rainforest reached down the mountain to cover the foothills rising up from the tropical lowlands. This part of the Kirrama Range traditionally belonged to the Girramay people and was loaded with waterfalls.

Although green ants plopped onto the picnic table with moderately alarming frequency, much of my time there was peaceful. The constant rain, mostly a permanent mist that managed to soak my clothes within a few minutes of leaving the car or the tent, kept other campers away.

The low-level roar of the falls reached all the way to the camping area. The sound made for a soothing afternoon lullaby punctuated by the calls of birds well hidden in the thick canopy.

After pitching my tent and arranging my gear, I explored the sections of the stream marked as swimming holes. Both were small and relatively shallow but would have offered a refreshing dip if I hadn't already been soggy.

A single hiking trail led up a short but steep path to a lookout point. From there the cascade was clearly visible. The water churned into white fluff that bumbled over tiers of black rock edged with moss. The chutes carved by the flow gouged the rock deeply as if the water sought to return to Earth's womb.

Out over the treetops, the rays of the sun separated the fog into rainbow colors. The gossamer mist settled onto the ridge like a novice on horseback, gingerly, gently. The area beneath the canopy was already murky; the sun was setting and I had to head back before I lost the light needed to follow the narrow path.

Dusk has always been a magical time. Something about the rapid change of light shifts the world closer to a different dimension. The borders that seem so clear in the sun's glare become murky. One thing blends into the other, creating strange shapes and wondrous beasts.

My journey back down took me through a nearly magical realm. Trees that had sprung from clusters of rocks entangled the stones with roots. Their trunks were wreathed with liana vines that climbed toward the elusive sun. The thickening air faded into gray, and the drip of water animated the jungle's leaves.

I was tangled in the miracle of this place, the continent as a whole and this particular area. The rainforest was an endless movement between known and unknown, a collection of thousands of living things that merged into one immense, breathing whole.

I was feverish with delight, nearly delirious. I threw my arms wide to embrace the world, to clutch the air itself, to cycle this wellbeing through my bones and back into the land.

Grandfather

THE NEXT MORNING, I clambered back to the falls with my camera. The smells were sensual and overpowering: the tangy richness of rotting wood, the pinching pulse of a fermenting stream bed, the red-wine fertility of black, heavy compost.

I donned my swimmers and wandered down to one of the pools. The forest towered and pressed. On either bank, matted green moss met the swollen crystal stream. For the rest of the day I lazed in the jungle with one ear tuned to the cockatoos croaking overhead.

That night, I tucked into my sleeping bag as usual. Two other campsites were occupied but we were all separated enough to provide a sense of solitude. The roar of the falls and the sound of the stream overrode much of the human noise. I had planned to stay there a few more days and was pleased that the place was so quiet.

After only a few hours, I jolted awake and sat up straight. Terror clogged my throat. Someone or something was nearby, was *too* near; I felt with a certainty beyond logic that danger lurked outside the tent.

I heard nothing more than the usual sounds of water and jungle...no footsteps or snapping twigs, no rustle of clothes or other human activity. Still my lungs pulled at the damp air, still my eyes stared wildly as if my gaze could pierce the tent walls.

With an unthinking smoothness, I flipped the sheath from the knife. The rough hilt warmed quickly in my palm, and the deadly stinger promised to match whatever enemy might appear. My gut was icy-hot, the night felt empty and cold. The rushing cataract had turned hollow and ill. Panting, I waited to fight for my life.

As suddenly as the terror had struck, it melted away. The spirit of my grandfather appeared and swaddled me with warmth. I felt his presence as surely as if he was still alive. His sheltering comfort charged the space around me with a golden barrier. The dark one moved away for that night, at least.

Early the next morning, I packed my gear and left. I would not tempt the violent shadows through more dark hours.

To this day I cannot say whether the danger was human or not. I only know that throughout my life, I have escaped situations that have wounded or scarred many others. For a long time, I had attributed that good fortune to all the prayers my parents sent up for my brother and me. In Australia, a budding connection with divine grace had become my protector.

Careless Breaths

AT A LAYBY where campers could pull off the highway outside Gordonvale, horses and cattle grazed near a raised railroad trestle. A woman flung wide her trailer door, hung out a sign for a barber shop, and enjoyed a brisk trade throughout the afternoon.

Enormous trees sheltered me from the sudden downpours but couldn't protect the fire. Deserting the meager coals, I gnawed undercooked potatoes and watched the bay fill beyond capacity.

Morning brought the hesitant twitters of a few birds and the intermittent splatter of water rolling from one leaf to another. A hacking cough preceded a rickety older man as he spindled toward me. He leaned heavily against the car until the spasm passed.

"I've got a nice fire going," he wheezed. "Thought you might like to cook something or warm up a bit."

I gathered my supplies slowly to allow the man a head start. His cigarette goaded the harsh cough with every puff. Balanced side by side on a log, we watched cars shake the highway awake with lazy, sporadic movements. As the bread toasted and the water boiled, my companion waved me to a small cooler. I folded back a cloth that had replaced the lid to find a dish of butter, jam, and a jar of milk.

The man shared comments that were as wandering and untamed as his iron-grey hair. He'd noticed a particular pair of campers who circled the coast every few months, likely following jobs from city to town. Then he pointed at one of the several busses in the parking bay.

"That tour guide," he said, "is ripping off the customers. They probably charged for accommodation and then brought 'em out here to camp."

His laughter disintegrated into a fit of coughing. I rose to flip the bread and added instant coffee to the water. My companion preferred tea and the last of his smoke.

"Them in the Kombi poked their heads out last evening," he said. "Seems they're doing the big tour, out to see the whole country. But they don't do nothing but sit in the van all night. I'd not like that. This is my country. I want to die out here."

He lit another cigarette.

"Don't be afraid of me," he blurted. "I wouldn't try anything, no, not me. I just like to talk, see. And even if I tried something then all you'd have to do is thump my chest and down I'd go. Not much longer for it, not me."

I brushed crumbs from my lap and rolled the morning's first cigarette. The smoke curled through the moist air, carrying with it another minute, another hour. Even as I puffed, I vowed to quit. I had broken so many habits that were killing my spirit but had forgotten about those careless breaths. To discover myself doing so foolish a thing next to a dying man ogled me with surprise.

A Helping Hand

MY NEXT STOP WAS Innot, a tiny town where a caravan park and spa had been built next to hot springs. For a few orgiastic days, I padded through the early morning mist to indulge. Cows that had passed the night on the warm sands hoisted up and away at my approach. The ground steamed like creamy pitch, and in the quiet preternatural scene I awaited the thunderous footfalls of dinosaurs.

As I built a small cook fire that evening, an older man appeared on the long path to my site. He shouted good evening from the hilltop and began speaking long before he drew near enough for me to hear his words.

"...and I saw you down in the springs all day," he said as he halted.

He braced one fist on his hip and leaned forward to await my reply.

"Oh, I'm really enjoying this," I said. "Especially after a few weeks in the rain."

"Up in the tablelands, were you?"

"Yeah. Felt sort of mildewed. But a good soak took care of that."

"Name's Cob. I work here, do maintenance and night patrol in exchange for rent. Thought I'd check on you down here by yourself."

We shook hands and he returned to his comfortable tilt. He gazed at me for a long moment before pushing off to return up the hill. As he moved away, he glanced back over his shoulder.

"You sure do fill out those swimmers right nice," he called.

Then he was gone, moving up the hill and back to his chores.

All the next day, when I wasn't wallowing in the spring, I wallowed in the thermal spa. The bubbles were amusing but a bit enthusiastic so I paddled from one side to the other. A blue-winged kookaburra skimmed the pool, dipping its head to catch dribbles of water on its back before roosting on the fence.

"I seen you walking by," Cob called as he unlatched the gate. "I brought you this."

He handed me a puffy silver bag with a white spout.

"Well, thanks," I said.

He lounged expectantly, clearly waiting for me to use my new toy.

"Um," I said. "What is it?"

"It's the bladder from a wine box. You know, those liters you throw in the fridge? After you empty it out, a puff or two of air turns it into a right nice pillow for when you're in the water!"

I thanked him and watched his gaze caper over my legs.

"You sure do fill out them swimmers nice," he said.

He turned to leave, levering himself halfway around before looking back to confirm his appraisal. "Right nice," he said.

Cob continued to be helpful during my stay, mostly by appearing at unlikely times to tell me how well I filled out my swimmers. If an American man had done the same I would have been miffed. But this was Australia where chauvinistic guys were part of the mythos. How could I be anything but amused by these living stereotypes, these men so forthright with their appreciation of my body and so unsuspecting of my inner strength?

American Dreaming

THE BARKLY HIGHWAY had been built on a wide, flat plain that flooded during the wet. The rainwater would sluice beneath a roadbed built at ground level and wash away the pavement, so the highway ran atop a ridge that was about five feet tall.

The strip was narrow, a single lane in each direction edged with a narrow shoulder. Despite its elevation, the pavement had buckled during freezing nights and boiling days.

Drivers, myself included, straddled the dividing line to avoid the crumbling edges. Whenever a car approached from the other direction, the vehicles pelted toward each other and swerved into their own lanes only when a collision was imminent.

Chugger raced along like an aged greyhound whose heart was large but whose limbs were unsteady. By that point, barely four months into my journey, I had covered more than half the 18,000 miles I would eventually trace along that *National Geographic* map.

The car was showing the wear from the demands I had placed on it as well as those times it had faithfully served other tourists. The front end squeaked and the steering pulled noticeably to the left. Chunks of bonding material had sheared away, and the carpet supported more weight than the perforated floor pans.

The Ford also pitched heavily on a suspension that had deteriorated badly. The wavelike bobbling made the car harder to manage on rough roads but racing down the smoother middle portion wasn't terrible.

Then, as Chugger tickled its maximum safe speed, the right rear tire blew. The car wobbled from the shoulder to the oncoming lane as I struggled for control. When the crumbling edges of the pavement delivered a particularly jarring thump, the car was thrown off the raised highway.

Launched from that height, we soared through the air. Chugger landed with a thump, fortunately on all four rims, and continued to bounce over rocks and shrubs. The terrain, the jouncing, and the speed made it unsafe to steer or hit the brakes. All I could do was hold the car steady.

The steering wheel jittered as the leaping settled into short hops fueled by a careening momentum. Even as the hops dissipated, the suspension was unable to quell the wild pitching. Directly ahead stood a lonely tree, a twisted, thick mallee. There wasn't a damned thing I could do to avoid ramming it.

I sank into the seat as if that might prevent my head from crashing through the windshield. I was preternaturally aware of my body, the car, and that tree. The brittle vinyl upholstery was crackly and slick beneath my thighs. The seat's springs pressed into my back every time the car bottomed out. The windscreen was filmed with dust, just as my eyes had been in that dream vision of my lonely corpse.

I was going to die. I knew that as surely as I knew my own name, and with that knowledge came a strange sort of despair. It felt weepy and dreamy, as if I was mourning at the funeral of someone I missed terribly while accepting that the loss was final. A tight thread of fear sparked the grief with bright electric shocks.

Then a crystalline clarity bloomed in my soul, and with it came a different kind of knowledge. This was not what I wanted. I did not want to leave my lifeless form beneath that tree, I did not want to die just yet.

My mind washed clean and my muscles relaxed. I looked at the highway streaming by on the right and thought: That's where I want to be. One hand twitched the wheel, hoping that the small adjustment wouldn't flip the car. And just like that, the Ford was ripping along the highway.

I don't remember turning the wheel far enough to head toward the road. There are no memories of angling the car so that the bumper wouldn't dig into the steep slope of the roadbed. I don't recall mounting the pavement and adjusting quickly so as not to fly off the other side. All I know is that the decision was made, my wrist twitched, and with a blink, the car was back on the highway.

I pulled onto the thin shoulder and sat there for long minutes. Adrenaline left me trembling and gasping. In the rearview mirror, I spotted the tire tread that had peeled away and sent me flying toward death. On the left, the twisted mallee dripped silent pools of shade. I averted my gaze.

Eventually I was able to roll a shambled cigarette but still didn't trust my legs. When the cigarette was half gone, a truck veered around the thrown tread and stopped behind the Ford. The driver trotted over to and asked if I needed help.

"Good thing you didn't go off the road," he said.

"I did."

I stopped speaking when he shook his head.

"No way you went off the road," he said. "Not in this thing. If you had, this car would have flipped. You'd be dead."

I didn't try to convince him otherwise. As we changed the tire, he continued to remark on how lucky I had been. Several times he scanned the desert, possibly looking for tracks. He found nothing but that didn't change what had happened.

As he drove away, I took a final look around. Just as I had dreamed, the tree stood alone. But my journey through the Outback had changed me. I was no longer the person I had been before arriving in Australia. I was no longer the woman who had dreamed her own death. My corpse would not lie alone in the grassland.

Frog Juice

FARTHER NORTH, storms didn't occur often enough to fill the rain tanks travelers relied on for water. The government had therefore sunk bores and installed windmills to pump the water up from underground.

A jug set out overnight ensured a refreshingly chilled morning drink. Even though I covered the jugs with damp towels, by noon the water had grown warm enough to make the mineral flavor unbearable. Gulping only a few ounces made me gag, so drinking enough to avoid dehydration was a challenge.

I scratched through the trunk and stumbled upon a jar of Tang, food of astronauts and desert rats alike. An avalanche of the vibrant powder almost disguised the sediment. I pretended the grit was undissolved powder; when that failed to be convincing, I told myself that I ate more dirt with my baked veggies every evening.

Native species had developed survival traits to address these kinds of issues. The water-holding frog could wait underground for up to seven years for rain. If no other water could be found, the tribal people knew how to find the frogs' burrows. A firm squeeze coaxed the creature to relinquish a beverage that surely tasted better than bore water.

As I chewed my water before dying embers, bats squealed above and rats rustled nearby. The rodents boldly scrabbled at the stony ground around my feet. One pair rattled pans and plates while a third dove under the tent. Perhaps it was hunting the tasty scorpions that so enjoyed sheltering beneath my tent.

As I headed into the Top End, the heat grew relentless. The sun leached all color from the earth and the humid air curdled. Around dusk when the furnace began to cool, I approached a faucet with my nearly empty water cans.

One tiny problem stood in the way. Well, really it was hundreds of tiny problems: green ants.

Although ants usually derived all the water they needed from their prey, in certain conditions they needed to drink. The weaver ants swarmed up the pipe and over the handle to sip from a slow leak. I waved my hand to scare them off but they took no prisoners. They strained toward my fingers with scissoring pinchers. *Just one sting, please, sweet Jesus!* they cried.

I waved a stick near the bottom of the pipe hoping to draw the troops away from the faucet. No luck. But a waggling fork sent them into a rage, and the battalion rushed down the pipe. I twisted the tap twice before they scurried back to the handle. Once the jug was topped off, the fork infuriated them long enough for me to close the tap. After two twists, the ants reclaimed the handle.

If the little bastards ever learn to jump, mankind can kiss its sweet ass goodbye.

A Manly Yarn

MY STOCKS WERE READY for a long stay inside Kakadu National Park. Not far past the entrance, a shallow lake spread like a melted silver dollar. Magpie geese and ibis mingled with cranes that combed the marsh. Their calls twined into a clamor that filtered across the water.

Obiri Rock, a deep overhang in the northeast corner of the park, had sheltered Aboriginal people during the wet. Generation after generation had drawn on the walls and ceiling and, once the blank areas had been filled, layered portraits atop the older ones.

The ever-popular barramundi were clearly distinguishable from the catfish. Mullet heads were snapped back to indicate that their necks had been broken. Snake-necked turtles, made tasty by a high concentration of fat, vied for space with the occasional kangaroo.

One drawing depicted the thylacine, the Tasmanian tiger, complete with stripes across the flanks. Believed extinct since the 1930s, the wolf-like marsupial had occasionally been sighted. I liked to think that such unusual creatures survived in the rugged belly of Oz where rainbow tales came true.

A human form drawn like a stick figure was attributed to the Mimi, spirit people with supernatural powers. The Mimi could fly and walk through rock, and drew pictures in places no human could reach.

A shallow outcropping captured a Mimi-style battle sparked after a girl had been punished too severely. Superimposed atop this scene were the Namarakain, unearthly sisters who occasionally mutated into crocodiles and ate anyone who wandered by. The Pandanus or screw palms at the head of the nearby river had sprung up after the sisters had planted their victims' teeth like seeds.

Although art was scattered all over the park, the Anbangbang shelter offered the most impressive gallery. Paraffin ledges over many of the pictures diverted runoff and lessened the effects of erosion. Traditionally a fading image would be repainted by the next generation, and some art had withstood the centuries.

Namarrkon the thunder spirit stood out due to his enormous eyes. Lightning bolts zigzagged from his head to his feet, and the stone hatchets that created thunder sprang from his elbows and knees.

Nearby was the spirit that punished female criminals by striking their heads with a yam. A rather impressive set of genitals dangled between his legs.

"Punisher of women," mused a man at my elbow. "I reckon he's scary enough but a yam? What do you think?"

"I'm not sure," I said, "but it might be a euphemism."

Fifty Million Bushflies

AT SOME POINT, the car was invaded by tiny black ants. The swarms crawled through the engine compartment, marched busily around the inside fender, and breached the panel behind the dash. As I drove away, I assumed that they would decamp the next evening.

Unfortunately the horde decided that the stuffing inside the front seat was a perfect new home. The throngs teemed over my legs but were harmless. Even though they tickled and itched, the prolific bushflies had made me immune to such minor irritants.

To a certain degree, anyway. Kakadu provided the perfect environment for the pests. Water buffalo survived quite well on the lush aquatic plants, which in turn allowed the dung-feeding bushfly to flourish.

While I had learned to live with them in the desert, the numbers amassed in the Northern Territory created an onslaught. Waking to the soft light scented by gum trees, I could already detect the first faint thrum of gossamer wings. And I'm not talking fairies.

I rolled my sleeping bag and packed everything precisely before unzipping the screen. The moment the door opened, flies poured in. The few steps from the tent to the car found me covered with hundreds of bugs slightly smaller than the common European housefly.

Experts, flyologists, I assumed, said that they clung so tenaciously because they were waiting for more of their favorite food. Unlike the less fibrous dung of carnivorous dingoes and the dry pellets of water-conserving roos, human excrement was well structured and moist.

Apparently a bushfly child could ask for no finer a nursery, and bushfly parents were devoted enough to chase their nursery providers to the ends of the earth. Repellant only prevented them from landing for more than a second. They crawled into my ears and flew unerringly up my nostrils, perhaps hoping for a bit of shade.

Attempts to squash the maddening things or at least shoo them away became a ridiculous dance. Once, driven to the edge, I shouted, "Piss off!" and flapped all my limbs. That drew the stares of nearby campers. Apparently my neighbors though my demand was meant for them because they moved their trailer onto the dirt track about half a kilometer away.

I was too entrenched in the battle to notice. I erected a mosquito net. The bushflies squeezed through the weave, leaving their larger horsefly cousins despondently attached to the exterior. Meals could only be protected by laying a bandanna atop the food; even then, the bushflies sucked the juices through the thin cloth.

I finally struck a compromise. I only waved them off when they landed on my face. They were free to congregate unmolested on any other part of my body. Relatively peaceful meals were secured by setting scrapes or a small portion of my food on the ground.

Even after resigning myself to hauling about a few pounds of bushflies, I wanted nothing more than a very large lizard to perch on my shoulder and pick off the airborne fanatics. Alas, even the giant goanna wasn't was that hungry.

I walked with my head down and my eyes squeezed into slits as if a heavy rain poured from the sky. Indeed there was a reign, the reign of the flies, and I was lord.

Crocodile Snack

KAKADU'S SANDSTONE PATHWAY wound through valleys of sedimentary rock. The flaky edges stacked up like delicate pastry dough trimmed with pinking shears. Black cockatoos embalmed beneath their monkish cowls lined a barren tree. The landscape was still, reflecting the motionless state my mind had achieved.

The parched earth supported scattered trees and little scrub. Kapok or silk-cottonwood trees survived well there. Nearly all had shed their leaves to produce a yellow flower and a brown pod. Most of the pods had already split open, spilling the puffy cargo that disbursed the seeds.

In other areas, Kakadu was lush. I trod a marsh that catered to the magnificent jabiru, a black-necked stork. A snakebird, a relative of the cormorant, spread its wings like an Egyptian hieroglyph. Blue-grey brolga cranes wore a patch of red that wrapped from their yellow beaks to behind their heads.

My feet kicked up puffs of dust that knit themselves into a smoky scarf. Clumps of dried grasses were scattered like sheaves of wheat. I was inside the landscape, I had become a part of nature. I could fly the mist caves formed by clouds, I could plunge into the packed soil as easily as if it was water.

Night brought the blessed coolness, the sky donned sequins, and fruit bats ventured among the trees. The leathery creatures fluttered and twitched and unfurled their wings like origami animated by the breeze. Their squabbles provided quite a bit of entertainment during the day.

Nights were tinted with menace. Campers were warned not to settle within fifty meters of any waterway because saltwater crocodiles had been known to hunt inland during lean times. Of course, any animal capable of walking 150 kilometers to find water wouldn't be deterred by another few meters.

Several jittery evenings passed as their growling roars sounded along the streams. One evening I heard the thrashing of something being dragged beneath the cold lilies. The kerosene lantern was not nearly bright enough and the batteries for the flashlight had gone dead.

The idea of sleeping in the car crossed my mind more than once. Although the rear seat was uncomfortable, it would have provided a safe refuge. But the decision involved more than safety and comfort. The unseen creatures pressing so near were as terrifying as the boogeyman. If I caved before an unlikely danger, what other fears might be allowed to take over?

The Pleiades sparkled overhead. The constellation represented seven Aboriginal sisters who had insisted on enduring the same initiation ceremonies as the boys. After they faced many frightening ordeals, they became women.

My self-imposed initiation, this journey through a land both harsh and breathtaking, demanded that I master my own fears. A hungry crocodile would mean my end. There would be no sprint to safety, no fighting off a one-ton predator with a buck knife. Yet I could not bring myself to sleep in the car.

I had not come this far by cowering in safe places. The tent was shelter enough, and every evening I swept the darkness for glowing amber eyes less often.

Sea Snake

AS I SKIRTED the Kimberly Region's southern end, the heat continued unabated. I lazed away the afternoons under boab trees almost as thick as the car was long but even their dense shade provided little relief. I had long abandoned warming the water used for my shower. Breezes were rare and the wind was either gale-force or nonexistent.

Swilling the inevitable cup of tea, travelers crouched in the dust to enjoy what little shade their vehicles cast. The water grew more saline as I approached the coast and instant coffee could not kill the taste. Often the desalination plants run by roadhouses were improperly operated, and I avoided drinking too much for fear of becoming ill.

Whenever I chanced upon fresh water, usually from supplies hauled to the roadhouses by tankers, I topped off my containers. The fresh was reserved for drinking and the desal served for washing, an aggravating endeavor. Detergents refused to foam and cleaning anything required gobs of soap and plenty of patience. My clothes degenerated from hopeless to laughable. At least everything matched.

Cable Beach, a clothing-optional area near Broome, offered some relief. The beach was accessible to vehicles, so I parked near a cliff and stripped as the drivers of a few 4WD trucks pretended to baby their vehicles over the sand. Even though the plastic lawn chair sucked at my cheeks whenever I shifted, the afternoon promised to be pleasant.

The amount of sunscreen required to cover parts of my body that had not felt the sun since puberty was enormous. I stealthily observed the men in anticipation of the moment when they would reapply sunscreen. How could they protect their equipment and still be polite?

Would they apply cream quickly or rub it in well? And the question that burned brightest: would that special limb require a higher SPF?

My questions were never answered, so I cavorted in the surf. I had no swimsuit to slip down or bunch up, no binding built-in bra, no constricting leg holes. With each wave, sand scoured my skin. Intimate, tingly bubbles rose along my pudendum, up my belly and over my breasts. The effervescence clung to my nipples like a thousand sparkling kisses.

Then I spotted the largest sea snake ever bumping a fellow's leg. But I must have been mistaken because the guy was nowhere near the water.

Guerilla Travel

AS DUSK FELL AT KARRATHA, a family invited me to join them at their picnic table. The mother broke out a bag of potato chips while I loaded the kids with pastry. The shiny, polite children wriggled often but remained quiet. My contemplation of their eerie goodness was interrupted by the father.

"I'm taking the family through the Kimberly," he said, "and around the Top End. I'm about to sell the truck and want the children to have a real bush experience first."

I glanced at the gear piled atop and around the truck but didn't see any extra wheel rims or petrol cans. The area he would travel was very remote, and most people who went on those kinds of trips packed so as to be self-reliant. The father seemed to depend more on bonhomie than common sense.

I told him about the couple I'd met near Camooweal, the ones who'd been waiting for car parts to arrive. During one of their trips, the wet season had begun early. The track had turned into a bog, and they hadn't dared to pull over because they knew they would be stuck for good.

Despite their best efforts, the van slid into a pit of mud. Days passed before a lone roo shooter came along and used the winch on the front of his truck to pull them out. Their rescuer led them to a cattle station where they sat for a week waiting for the road to dry out.

That same year, another couple who had bogged down lived in their van for some time. They were the last vehicle to travel that road for six months. Eventually the food gave out, and neither of them knew how to forage or hunt. Starvation killed the woman before claiming the man.

The father was politely attentive as he indulged these secondhand tales but dismissed any notion that the same might happen to him. Then a hulk of a man appeared. He was part of a special Australian military force trained in guerilla tactics and bushcraft skills.

“I heard about your trip,” he said. “Thought I’d see if you needed any advice.”

The picnic table creaked as he dipped his whiskers into the rippling light of the lantern. He spread out a handful of battered maps and traced the route the family would take with one stubby finger.

“I see you’re taking your kids,” he said. “Keep a close eye on them. They can disappear in a flash in that thick brush. And don’t let them touch nothing, either. You know about the stinging gimpy bush?”

“Oh, yes, of course,” Papa said.

“How about the caustic bush? It’s a tender looking thing but if the sap gets on you, it burns like acid. And for god’s sake don’t eat anything even if you’re lost. Half the stuff will kill you right off and the other half will kill you slow.”

Papa’s smile froze.

“And,” the man said, “stay clear of the black country, the black dirt. Just a little moisture bogs you to the axles. Buy a winch. In fact, buy two. You ought really to have another truck along to help you out of scrapes but a spare winch should do. And you’ll be wanting wheel rims as well as extra tires. Remember that the wet starts in a month, I reckon sooner this year, the worst time to travel the Top End.”

This land, grand and temperamental, could not be taken for granted. Papa’s joviality had crumbled a bit with each item missing from his supplies and each unrealized danger. He tried to dispel the doom by recounting stories with happier endings. Then, as he watched his children tumble into bed, doubt flickered in his eyes.

Please Don't Squeeze the Dolphins

GREY HUMPS MOVED through the waves and three dolphins lingered near the shore. In Monkey Mia, Western Australia, wild dolphins voluntarily interacted with humans every day. I moved along the beach until moist sand chilled my feet.

A woman whose nose was frescoed with white zinc scowled from beneath her Gilligan hat. "You're not allowed in the water until the rangers arrive," she said.

"Yes, I know," I said easily. "Thanks."

I turned back as a dolphin leapt for the sky.

"I said, you're not allowed in the water yet," the woman said in a testy tone.

"I'm not *in* the water," I replied in an equally testy tone.

I had risen at dawn to witness the first feeding and was not companionable before my caffeine fix, so I certainly wasn't prepared to be polite to some self-appointed hall monitor. When a second dolphin breached, the people lounging on the sand rose as one and approached the waves.

Ms. Zinc shot the first few dirty looks and then decided she didn't want to be left behind. Creatures of land faced creatures of water, and for a few minutes a reverential stillness swathed the crowd. Children giggled and adults whispered but magic danced in the air.

"Good morning," intoned the ranger as he waded into the ocean. "Please remain where you are while I go over a few simple rules. We don't have many but they are important."

He shifted the heavy bucket of fish from hand to hand as he asked us to keep our feet still. The mud along the shallow shoreline smelled pretty bad, and the dolphins didn't like murky water. We were told to move forward no further than where he stood to avoid the deadly spines of stonefish.

"Finally," he said, "don't touch the dolphins, let them touch you. Most dolphins do not like being touched. If a dolphin wants to be touched, it will come to you. And don't touch during a feeding. They have teeth and they will bite. They have bitten people before and they'll do it again. Remember, *they do not like being touched.*"

I thought that the ranger's weariness stemmed from having to repeat the same lecture several times a day. I rapidly discovered that his weariness sprang from the behavior he had come to expect from the human visitors.

Frowns quickly replaced smiles as the crowd jockeyed for better positions. The patience of the adults evaporated long before that of their children. The mob scene was compounded by the fact that the tour bus group would stay for only one show.

"Don't touch the dolphins," the ranger chanted, "let the dolphins touch you."

The dolphins occasionally rubbed a leg or responded to the ranger's voice with clicks and whistles. They used their snouts to splash the visitors and nodded wildly before rolling away. For the most part, however, they were busy dodging people.

Even with the ranger present, the crowd was only nominally contained. I was repeatedly shoved from behind. When I lost my balance and pitched forward, a woman snapped at me for having moved my feet.

Finally the ranger herded everyone back to shore. As the people moved away, the pod advanced. The ranger then chose individuals, mostly children, to hand a single small fish to the dolphins. With every selection, he repeated his mantra. One woman leaned down and patted a passing form.

"Don't touch!" the ranger barked.

Moments later he exploded again as a child followed the adult's lead. When the fish ran out, the buckets were upended to show the dolphins that snack time was over. Seconds later they were gone. Except for the enchantment shining from a few young eyes, the magic had long since disappeared.

Razor Fish

ON THE SAND DUNES around Shark's Bay, ice plants known as pigweed bloomed yellow flowers that were as bright as the sun. Red hills blown in from the desert set off the white dunes, and dingoes darted through the low scrub. A tiny grave hugged by rusted barbed wire marked the resting place of a child who had died in the 1800s. High above, galahs kept a silent vigil.

I returned to camp to watch a family dig up the elongated shells of razor fish, a name that reflected their tendency to shred unwary feet. The children filled bucket after bucket. Never one to pass up a free meal, I kidnapped three for myself. The shells were longer than my hand and smelled deliciously of the sea.

Back at camp, a woman struggled desperately to assemble a tent supported by a complex weave of guy wires. As I went over to offer help, three Danes charged to the rescue. Each was a study in a different shade of blond, and each was more handsome than the last. Then, of course, I *had* to help.

"Here's the directions," the woman said. "But they don't make much sense."

"Uf!" huffed one Dane cheerfully. "We are not needing those."

While the fellows worked, I struggled to decipher the instructions. They clearly had been translated from Aramaic into Egyptian hieroglyphs before being torturously written in English.

"Ho-kay!" crowed one of the men. "Let go!"

They released their corners, and the tent promptly keeled over.

"It is no worries," he said. "We try again."

Each grabbed a pole or a rope. The tent levitated like a weary phantom.

"No, no," the woman said. "That goes—"

"Let go!"

The men stepped back. The tent stood proudly for a moment before collapsing like a stranded jellyfish.

"Ah. Yes," the now deflated fellow said. "Where is manual, please?"

The trio studied the instructions for several minutes. With a sigh, the enthusiastic one tossed the paper over his shoulder. They gathered around the tent, no wiser but refreshed by the break. After more fiddling, they stepped back.

"Quickly!" one said. "Run away before it falls!"

In exchange for their effort, the woman offered to cut their hair. The camp kitchen served as an impromptu barber shop, and the shaggy trio emerged freshly shorn just before the dinner rush. Once the crowd had finished cooking, I carried my exciting new meal over to the hairdresser for any suggestions she might have for their preparation.

"Cor, those things are disgusting!" she said. "You're awfully game to eat something that looks like that on the outside. I can only imagine the inside is worse!"

If only I had heeded her words. I slit the small center muscle and sifted the foul-smelling innards for something that resembled an oyster. Blood flooded the counter, and the pile of organs oozed toward the sink. As I wondered whether I would eat that evening, the hairdresser glanced over my shoulder.

"Ugh!" she said. "You want some of my sausage instead?"

I politely declined and poked at my meal, casting about for that joker who had proclaimed razor fish edible. Just then the Danes came back and honed in on the gory mess. They marched over, dipping on eager legs like galleons leaping swells.

"You are eating this?" one cried before he smiled sweetly. "Are you sure that is enough?"

"I see dead thing on beach today," the second one said. "Perhaps you like to eat that also?"

Eventually some kind soul volunteered a crucial piece of information: the edible part was the minuscule muscle I had discarded with the shells. The remaining pound of green and purple flesh was garbage.

I swept the viscera into the bin and eagerly accepted a portion of the Danes' more pleasantly scented meal. Stir fry had never tasted better.

Car Park

MY RETURN TO SYDNEY led directly into the dark and suffocating bowels of the King's Cross car park, the area where travelers resold their cars. For months my only clock had been the rising of the sun and moon, the sinuous cycles of light and dark. Now exhaust and fluorescent lighting rudely reacquainted me with the modern world.

Chugger's engine had been rebuild and the five original tires had all blown and been replaced, so the price was a bit above what I had paid. By the third day, I dropped that number a hundred bucks every hour. My goal was to escape early enough to enjoy the city.

A French fellow waffled for a bit, and at AU$900.00 I threw in the tent. He countered with AU$800.00 and a ride back to the hostel, and we shook hands. As he trotted off to the bank for the rest of the cash, I waved the deposit at the three Danes who had shown up a day before I had.

Even though they had already dumped their car, they had returned to frolic with other sellers from their homeland. They also received quite a bit of free beer whenever successful sellers shouted a round for their neighbors.

"Congratulations!" trumpeted one. "What to do with new fortune? Perhaps you buy more razor fish?"

A young couple interrupted our rave to point at my soon-to-be-former car.

"Does the market see many cars smaller than this?" they asked.

We shook our heads. An occasional compact came through but they weren't much good outside the cities.

"We're going through the middle," the man said, "and are looking for a small four-cylinder."

The Danes and I burst out laughing.

"Four cylinders," yapped one as his blond curls flapped. "That is no good. Not up the middle."

"You want big car," agreed the darkest Dane, a lad with hair the color of wet straw. "Six, eight cylinders. At least six."

"We don't want to buy your cars," the man said.

"My car's sold," I said.

"Yes, and so is ours," the first Dane said. "This is not our car. Our car is gone, *poof!* Is sold."

The man looked a little less suspicious but not entirely trusting. "Well," he said, "why would we want a big car?"

"Is hard drive up middle, hard on car. Four cylinder, it goes *chik! chik! chik!* and is dead like that, it cannot go in heat and dust. Unless you are mechanic. You are mechanic?"

The man shook his head.

"Then six cylinder. It is good, it lasts."

They argued for a few more minutes until Blondie shrugged. "Hokay," he sighed. "You choose. Is your life you risk, not mine."

The couple backed away, clearly convinced that we were as barmy as bandicoots.

Saying Goodbye

WITH NEARLY A FULL WEEK LEFT before my flight, I explored Sydney. The shops and row houses were brightly painted, and they rose and fell along the undulating streets like the ribbons on a jester's cap. Scooters in candy colors buzzed around the buses, adding their breath to the clouds of diesel exhaust. More than once I stared at airplanes overhead; the sight had become alien and unfamiliar.

The city had no natural rhythms. There was only the onslaught of rumbling lorries and snarling buses that grew louder every day. I wandered the streets feeling disjointed in my body and my soul. The days were pleasant yet somehow adrift. A holiday season with family awaited my return but parts of me felt as raw and exposed as if I was being ripped away from a twin.

Although I longed to see my family, I also wanted to sink into the peaceful red dust and the soothing green waters again. But I would not retreat. My time in Australia was done, and not simply because the visa would expire the day after my flight.

I had started this journey out of desperation. Depression, an oppressive corporate culture, my failure to begin my career as an author, and my inability to lift myself out of that rut had launched me—perhaps in a foolhardy way, perhaps in a way driven by instinct and an already strong connection to the divinity that resides in us all—into a world where timeclocks and schedules and productivity followed the rules of a primal mother. There I had found peace. There I had found the smallest part of myself, a piece that was stronger than iron and the best foundation upon which to build.

Now, that didn't mean I understood those changes when I boarded the return flight. It would take me ten years to circle back and close out the last of the Outback's lessons. And because I didn't truly comprehend the fullness of that internal shift, I didn't immediately apply much of what I had learned.

I had held my own in one way, however. After I had left Monkey Mia, the company I'd semi-abandoned started calling for me. Nearly two months were left on my itinerary but they contacted my parents repeatedly and asked them to pass along the news: they were finally ready to offer me that promotion!

But I had to return right away. If I continued with my sabbatical, they would fill the position with a new hire. I refused to cut my trip short. My entire life hadn't been rearranged just to lose whatever the additional time might offer.

The calls continued to arrive at my parents' home. The corporate gears continued turning and, as corporate gears will, they ground along with a languorous sloth matched only by the witchetty grub. When I finally reached Sydney, the position was still open. Surprise!

Another journey began. After landing in Los Angeles, I picked up the suit and dress shoes my mother had mailed to my friend in California. After one night at his place, I boarded a flight to Sacramento. Arriving directly from the airport, I slogged through a six-hour interview—which included a presentation I had put together during my final weeks overseas—then returned to Los Angeles that evening and flew out the next day for Virginia.

The interview had gone exceptionally well. Perhaps a dozen people from different departments met me at various times to chat about their expectations and mine. The position was a great opportunity, especially for someone whose degree didn't allow for much beyond writing or teaching. Technical editor? Sounded great!

Until the division head sat me down in his office and dumped a four-inch, ten-pound binder on the table. The report—which was substantial enough to have kicked up a draft when it landed—was the kind of thing I would be responsible for editing.

I would also manage the reports' production schedules and coordinate the contributions of all the individuals involved in researching, writing, and analyzing the reports. Each team would produce one of these reports every month, so my evenings and weekends would mostly belong to the company.

The moment that binder hit the table, my belly flopped around like a bucket of slime. *I don't want to do this,* I thought. But it was a great opportunity. It was what I had been reaching for, a huge leap into the lower layers of the managerial stratosphere and the first step toward a stratospheric income.

As an additional bonus, the job required that I transfer to California, a place where I'd always wanted to live. Lots of challenge, a funky West Coast lifestyle, plenty of great weather in which to cavort...what wasn't there to love? I took the job.

Less than ten months later, that decision caught up with me. And not only because of the corporate culture or the horribly long hours. The company I had felt so good working for was not exactly what it seemed.

Our clients consulted with the environmental engineers about producing fewer pollutants and cleaning up toxins dumped during unregulated decades. Instead of coaching high-minded companies that wanted to be responsible planetary citizens, the real goal was very different. The clients wanted to balance the cost of cleaning up pollutants against EPA regulations...that is, to save as much money as possible by cleaning up as little as possible.

The reports I produced contained equations that looked like Chinese calligraphy. Each of those equations was freighted with an immense gravity. They computed the "acceptable" number of birth defects, childhood diseases, cancers and deaths that would be caused by the waste that wasn't cleaned up. In essence, my company helped big polluters—mostly paper mills and government superfund sites—weigh money against the quality of human life.

As you might imagine, that made it hard to look at myself in the mirror every morning. So I cashed in my 401K and started writing. The first thing I wrote was this memoir, which won an award.

A few years later I began writing my first novel, *The Family Made of Dust.* The novel follows a biracial Aboriginal man stolen away from his family by Australia's genocidal regulations. That book won two national awards and was called "the best novel in ten years."

Despite the significant honor, the income didn't come close to what I could have made had I sacrificed my soul and everything I believed in. Yes, my choice to abandon the corporate ship required a different set of sacrifices. But that choice returned rewards far beyond what even the most complex equation could measure.

There in the red desert and the heat and the dust, my chrysalis had been shed. The world from which I had come, that self-made world with its soul-shredding job, was not the world into which I would settle. The choices and perceptions of others, the goals of the so-called good life had been left behind during that 18,000-mile trek.

In its place, I had formed a connection with the earth. While listening to its casual respiration, I had heard the pulse of my blood. My initiation had opened my heart.

Every day while I was in Sydney, I stopped on the green islands that floated atop the heaving concrete to feed the birds bread and fruit. The coos and screeches of pigeons and seagulls reinforced the flow of existence that is everywhere we seek for it.

Those wild creatures would be my touchstone in the journeys to come, a reminder that all the world flows toward its balancing point. What a wonderful blessing I had been given. What a joyful life I went on to build.

As a woman.

A woman alone.

Thank you for reading Woman Alone
A Sixth-Month Journey Through the Australian Outback.

Please leave a review on your favorite site.

A Free Sample From

Seven Sisters

Spiritual Messages From Aboriginal Australia

Desert Dreaming

SOME YEARS AGO, I spent six months camping alone in the Australian outback. Every night I cooked over an open fire as dingoes patrolled the bush. I heard the stories of travelers and citizens along with Aboriginal lore. The experience made me recognize new truths, some of which became clear only after I had returned to America.

One of those truths is that people haven't changed much for thousands of years. Planes and global commerce have replaced ponies and trade routes, yet still we struggle to put food on the table. The internet makes other nations our neighbors even as our careless words hurt people we love. None of our glorious technological advances have resolved the issues of the human heart.

Even changes that enhance our lives can cause trouble. The speed of progress demands ever-faster adaptations that leave some people feeling unbalanced. Extremists embrace bombs as "final solutions." The void between human rights and religious beliefs seems as large as ever. Meanwhile, the culture of celebrity buries meaningful experience beneath glittering photos and instant video feeds.

At its core, this chaos is neither bad nor good. It is only a symptom of growth. Our global society is a teenager searching for what it might become. Guidance comes from the elders, cultures that predate our multi-gig civilization. The parents of our modern age are the social and religious traditions that developed during the last few thousand years. Its grandparents are tribal and spiritual systems that are older still.

Throughout time and across all countries, the one constant has been our stories. Folktales told around the campfire have become movies lit by electric fire. Long ago, different versions were told to older listeners to help them tackle more complex issues. Films and books do the same by targeting youth or adults, Gen Y or boomers. As society changes, the details of our stories change. Since we are still dealing with the same challenges, though, the messages remain the same.

Our personal stories work the same way. Every time employees gather in the breakroom, they share tales from their lives. When we discuss the plot of a popular TV show, we share perspectives, teach lessons, and search for meaning. Movies, books and documentaries show us how other people think and live. Open video sites show us what we think about ourselves and how we want others to see us. On YouTube, Facebook and blog sites, we try out the roles of hero and antihero, villain and victim.

All these stories have little to do with tribes or nations and everything to do with being human. Each tale provides us with another solution to the riddle of how to be our best. We become patient with our relatives and ourselves; we forgive our enemies even when they are friends who have betrayed us. Every hero thrills by mirroring our own potential. Every villain chills by showing us the same.

Stories have always been an important part of our humanity. Our brains are hardwired to envision new lives and try out different perspectives. Our imagination spins wonderful tales while our logic registers the lessons. The process gives us a safe way to explore an unsafe world. Stories spark our greatest power, the ability to grow using only our minds.

Tales from Aboriginal Australia can transform us spiritually. Of course, the culture and geography of the Dreamtime are different than our own. Yet the messages and the essays that delve into those messages deal with everyday issues: illness and joy, victory and death, love and friendship. The original instructions were given to us all. We all seek peace within ourselves and harmony with others.

According to Australia's ancient cultures, all creatures and things emerged from the Dreamtime. The Dreaming is not just a collection of lore or a long-ago time; it is a living energy that flows constantly through the universe. It is then and now, divine and human, spirit and law. It teaches us how to survive in a harsh world and how to thrive in our souls.

Most clans conceived of a creation in which Earth already existed. Ancestors rose out of the ground and descended from the sky. Wherever their feet pushed up mounds, mountains arose; wherever the ancestors fought, the ground was trampled flat. Tribal members can still "read" the land by walking a story's path, its songline. In this way the people were connected to the land.

The largest songlines, epic stories of ancestors who ranged far across the continent, connected different tribes. When an ancestor crossed into new territory, the next part of the story belonged to the neighboring group. The entire songline could only be recited when all the tribes had gathered. Relationships between neighbors were therefore automatically—and spiritually—strengthened.

After walking those songlines myself, I returned to the United States with a very different perspective. My corporate job quickly imploded. I could no longer tolerate the gossip-ridden hallways, rules that were unevenly enforced, or that the environmental consulting firm was paid to assign monetary value to human life. And my fellow coworkers could not tolerate the negativity I had not yet purged from my soul.

I started anew as an author and spiritual messenger. As I offered the gift of Aboriginal folktales to others, messages from other cultures changed my perspective further. I started to become what I am today. I started to discover who I had been all along. My wish is that the stories in this book and the perspectives in the essays give you the same opportunity for growth, love, hope, and an abiding peace.

Walk with me now into the desert. Rocks jut out of the ground and everything is dusted in pink and red. Wiry clumps of spinifex grass sprout from the plain, and the purple flowers of bush tomatoes promise a sweet harvest. Smell the tang of eucalyptus trees and taste the cool water from a shady billabong. Hear the droning didgeridoo and the sharp click-sticks that accompany the songs. Take whichever Dreamtime messages will help you and your tribe as the gifts they are intended to be.

From the Heart of Love,

Laine Cunningham

EVERY ABORIGINAL GIRL looked forward to her initiation, the rites that would make her into a woman. Although the transition would be a happy time, the girls couldn't help but worry. They wondered if they would be able to learn all the songs and remember the lessons. Their bodies would know when the time had come and would make physical changes all by themselves. That knowledge gave the girls some comfort.

Boys underwent their own initiations, of course, frightening rites of blood and pain. Not every child succeeded the first time. When one boy failed the man-making ceremony, the shame was more than he could bear. To soothe his humiliation, he loudly claimed that girls were weak because their initiation wasn't nearly as difficult.

A young woman who had just completed her own rites grew angry at his words. Women's lives held dangers and pains no man could comprehend. Why, a mother had died in childbirth only the year before. Was she supposed to think less of the men because they would never face that danger? Ridiculous!

Still, the comments buzzed in her mind like a horde of bushflies. She wondered if other boys or even men thought the woman-making rite was less valuable. After fretting over this for days, she told her sisters something shocking. She was going to ask the elders to make her into a man.

The youngest sister, a reed-thin girl with hair like the floss of a kapok tree, began to cry. She thought the ceremony would actually change her sister's body into that of a man. Even after the others convinced her that wouldn't happen, she would not be silent.

The boys will say it's not fair to compare them to an adult, she said. *They must see that girls are also strong. I will go with you!*

For a long moment, no one spoke. Then it was agreed: If one went, they all went. What one suffered they would all suffer. The seven sisters had been that way ever since their mother had pushed them into the world like a living chain of years.

As they walked back to camp, they didn't say another word. Just by looking at the girls, everyone knew something serious was about to happen. Mothers put aside their grinding rocks and grandmothers scooped up the babies. Men stopped repairing their weapons, and even the boys abandoned their games to tag along. By the time the sisters stood before the elders, the entire camp had gathered.

The senior men and women knew the girls as wards to be cared for, as young minds that were curious yet lacking in experience. The oldest sister had already done much for her people so she was allowed to speak. When she did, the elders couldn't believe they had heard her correctly.

Test us with the man-making ceremony, the oldest sister said again. *Let us prove we are equal to men.*

For many hours the council discussed the request. Even as darkness grew, no one moved to light the fires or prepare food. Finally the senior woman nodded. Their request would be granted. As the oldest sister joined the ensuing celebration, she felt the eyes of the sky spirits on her. Her request was so unusual even they wanted to know if she would succeed. She could only hope that she would endure.

For the next few days, the girls' uncles disappeared for hours at a time. When they wandered back, they pretended not to have been gone while everyone else pretended not to have noticed their absence. One day the uncles left for only a short time. Then they leapt out of the bush shouting war cries.

The girls' mother and aunts grabbed the sisters in trembling arms. The men tugged and shoved intent on breaking the sisters free. It was time to change. Separating the children from everything they had ever known was the first step.

When the oldest sister's head was covered with a dingo pelt, she plunged into a darkness she'd never known existed. Each girl would face the ordeal alone. Hands guided them roughly into a fast run and the mourning cries of their aunts fell behind. For them, the girls were already dead.

By the time they reached the bora ground, the ceremonial site, their feet were bloody from thorns and stones. A man sang a song they had never heard before then told the girls to sing. They stammered as best they could through the chant. When the pelts were finally removed, the sisters saw seeds and stones arranged to form a symbol important to men.

The evening decayed into a dark night. The uncles left. For the first time, the girls weren't surrounded by aunties who could explain every sound and warriors who could defend against every enemy. If they lit a fire to drive away their fears, they would fail. If they fled the bora ground in terror, they would fail. If they attempted to return to camp, they would shame their family.

Strangeness haunted the dark hours. Terrible howls rose out of the bush and the sound of running feet mysteriously went nowhere. A sudden snap of branches startled the girls; a rhythmic clapping like boomerangs tapping together drove thorns into their temples. None of it made sense and all of it was terrifying.

When the sun finally rose, the uncles returned looking as rested as ever. The sisters were ragged and had bunched tightly together. The men lined them up and counted; seven remained. The girls had passed the first test. They had controlled their fear.

Training began in earnest. The men recited stories and songs that spoke of a man's life, his duties and his pride. The sisters stood motionless as their lips were cut over and over with a sharp stone. The sun wheeled through its burning cycle but they were given no food. Water was offered only at dusk, and then only what could be held in the palm of a man's hand.

After days of this, the uncles brought a feast. Bush tomatoes and bush potatoes and witchetty grubs had been roasted on hot coals. The loin of a kangaroo dripped with juice and the drumsticks of a bustard let off a smoky steam. Although their stomachs ached, the sisters took only enough to sustain their lives. In times of famine, their discipline would serve the entire clan. They had passed the final test.

The uncles used the sharp stones to scratch their own arms. They gathered up their blood and sprinkled it over the initiates as they sang the last song. The sisters had become men.

As they left the bora ground—this time without the cloak of youthful ignorance—everything looked different. They had a new path in the world and saw things from a different perspective. The oldest sister had felt much the same after her initiation into the world of women. Now she saw the world with the eyes of a man and a woman.

A corroboree, a celebration, was held in their honor. The oldest sister felt joy and pride. A part of her stayed detached, though, as if her soul moved in an entirely different realm. She yearned to transform again. Before that happened, she would be with her tribe for one more night...and then forever after.

Toward dawn, the corroboree was still going strong. The sun touched the horizon, yet the stars glowed like brilliant crystals. The sun climbed higher but the stars would not be quenched. Then the sky spirits swept the seven sisters into the heavens where they became a new constellation. To this day, the Pleiades remind us that men and women, although different, are equally strong.

WE OFTEN JOKE ABOUT DIFFERENCES between the genders to diffuse a very real tension. Men evolved to understand the world physically: to set aside emotions until they have the luxury of processing them, to spend long hours tracking in silence, to pursue and defend. Women evolved to understand the world intuitively: to communicate during group activities, to notice nonverbal signals from the youngest in their care, to select ripe berries based on years of ingrained experience. No wonder there's trouble!

In ancient times, the elder council eased the tension. Senior men discussed how events might affect the prosperity of the clan and other tribes. Senior women considered the emotional and psychological needs of individuals and the group. Every aspect of the community's physical and spiritual health was balanced against the others.

The seven sisters are extraordinary because they balanced different kinds of knowledge within themselves. They understood both masculine and feminine, physical and spiritual. When they added the pains of men to their pains as women, their wisdom surpassed that of the elders before their bodies had ripened enough to marry.

Taking on both male and female knowledge is dangerous. It requires one body and mind to bear the suffering of two genders. Yet sometimes that's exactly what women do...they carry their own burdens while shouldering those of a man. Single mothers protect and nurture their children while unmarried women build lives alone. Husbands grow ill or stumble so wives carry them for a month, a year, a lifetime. Widows become their own mates.

Today we are integrating the knowledge of the elder council, of both genders, into every level of society. Our schools and universities burst with female teachers and professors. Our businesses recognize the unique benefits of feminine leadership. Our highest courts understand that women from all backgrounds are wise, that their histories and experiences are critical to true justice.

Valuing women's perspectives has an additional benefit: it allows us to more fully value the contributions of men. In tribal structures, a man's reputation was based on what he did for the community. The best hunter and the highest earner provide no value if they hoard what they have hunted. Today, men who cannot achieve within a narrowly defined role are looked down on while "successful" men gobble up more than their share. Our modern society therefore does not truly honor a man's strengths and abilities.

When a man's identity is linked with iron chains to wealth or power, everyone suffers. Nations that focus only on tangible assets like economic stability and military strength lack the intangible assets of compassion and empathy. There is no use for grain stored in such vast quantities that it rots; there is no value to money horded in such quantities that it exists only as a numeric concept. A balanced society will distribute excess grain to those in need. A balanced person will utilize excess funds to bolster community projects.

The negative cycle of gender imbalanced is linked in other ways, too. When women's contributions are devalued, the man who performs the ultimate acts of strength—being a single father, carrying a wife through illness, allowing compassion to enhance his leadership—walks a gauntlet of social ridicule. He is "weak," "soft," "pussy-whipped," "gay." Gender-based terms make him womanly and therefore ineffectual. His strength is neutered by a brawny line between the sexes. *Approach that line,* men are told, *and become less than you were.*

The most important message from the Pleiades is that our natural state is one of mutual strength. The oldest sister did not want to physically become a man or to fulfill only a man's role. Nor did she seek to place women above men. Disenfranchising the men would have been as destructive as disenfranchising the women. Any society that values either gender more than the other is a society divided.

Back in the early days of the Dreamtime, the sisters were honored for their unique accomplishment. Despite having earned that respect, they had to be removed from the ancient world. Their dual perspective would have made their lives unbearable. Other women would not have been able to understand their knowledge of men; men would not have been able to relate to them as they did to other women. Their unique viewpoint would have caused the sisters an excessive amount of suffering.

Modern society has the opportunity to do what the sisters could not. During the last century, women and men have taken on each other's knowledge. Single parents, people who delay marriage or choose not to marry, widows and widowers have learned how to be protector and nurturer, provider and comforter. Now we can welcome people who hold this dual perspective. We can let their strength shine like stars burning among us.

This is the sacred message both genders have known since people first gathered into groups...that either gender can bear the burden for both. That the hearts of men and women are big enough and their arms are strong enough to carry a spouse, a family, a friend. This deeply spiritual love disappears only when we agree to hide it away. We are weak only when we choose to believe the modern myths that spring from issues of power and control, insecurity and instability.

These issues affect every nation in our modern world. In the U.S., much is made of the fact that religious restrictions in some countries bar women from receiving an education. Yet American fundamentalists from several popular religions bar women from becoming spiritual leaders or heads of household. Unwed mothers are maligned while absentee fathers, who conveniently bear no overt signs of their "sins," are spared any repercussions.

Our secular society is still influenced by these judgments. Education means little if it can never be used; employment is psychologically degrading when the wage gap between genders exceeds twenty percent; a woman making a bid for president is merely a footnote when few corporations have any female executives.

Yet the issue is not solely based in gender dynamics. Not when a college degree costs six figures, not when blue-collar workers are indentured by low wages and lower status. Domestic violence—against husbands and wives, children and elders—is driven in part by an economic model that pays too little for many people to support their families. The poorest among us are disenfranchised by a system that doesn't respect the contributions of every person.

Our societies have changed from tribes to nations, from neighborhoods to a global community. We are each responsible for improving our own society so it can improve the world. We are also responsible for sharing what we can with our far-flung neighbors. Our foreign sisters do not deserve fewer rights simply because they were born into systems mired in issues of power and control; our worldwide brothers also deserve to have their contributions fully valued.

In times of darkness, we need only look up to remember our power. The Pleiades, burning brightly for millennium, honor the sisterhood of mankind and the brotherhood of humanity. The way requires suffering, some of it harsh, and we will sometimes have to bear each others' burdens. Together we can celebrate equality and strength. Together we can lift free of our individual bodies. Together we can shine.

A Free Sample From

The Family Made of Dust

A Novel of Loss and Rebirth in the Australian Outback

1 The Precious Dead

WHEN A MAN DIES IN THE DESERT, he is completely alone. At thirty-nine, Ian McCabe knew this simple fact. He had spent most of his life working the demanding seasonal jobs that kept Australia's rural towns alive. He had seen a flat tire turn deadly, and knew that beauty and danger were the sisters who bore the land.

Ian was not a tall man but a shock of blond hair added inches to his height. Quick blue eyes and a steady aim were useful in his career as a kangaroo culler. Every night the slim .22 found its target between the shine of an animal's eyes. On cattle stations hundreds of kilometers wide, engine trouble and the bite of the brown snake posed constant threats.

Ian's white Land Rover was nearly twenty years old and it still ran like a lizard drinking—non-stop and practically unstoppable. In the rear a skillet, bedroll and a case of green beans were strapped onto narrow shelves. A bottle of port nestled in its own padded compartment, and a few golf clubs were tied to the wall. Sleep, slurp and sport, he called the collection, everything a man could want in one mobile space.

He eased the truck down the track. The spur was rough, really a strip of earth scraped clean of boulders, but it saved nearly half an hour. Besides, the less traveled a road was, the happier Ian felt. Cities, he knew, were for suckers. Why squeeze into a rabbit hutch when the outback was right next door?

This area, so close to the Davenport Ranges, was typical of the Northern Territory. Wide plains of twisted mulga trees reached southwest to Alice Springs. A network of creeks and rivers that ran only during the Wet sustained gum trees taller than most buildings. Cockatoos raised their young in the hollow trunks, and after a rain lorikeets gorged on the nectar in the blossoms.

Grass was sparse, edged out by the ubiquitous spinifex that cut flesh as cruelly as broken glass. Only the toughest creatures survived and half-feral Brahma cattle were the breed of choice. To a rancher beleaguered by drought and debt, every blade eaten by native animals robbed them of beef. Roo shooters were always welcome. And judging by the sun, Ian would arrive at the station house in time for dinner.

A flash of metal caught his eye. Through binoculars, he watched a red SUV beetle across the property. The truck stayed behind the ridges and moved slowly enough to keep its dust cloud low. The same stealth kept Ian from sight as he followed.

Eventually the trespassers parked beside a hill topped by a stone pinnacle. Ian stuffed the Land Rover under a mulga tree and watched as a pair of men hiked up the slope. The first, a sturdy white fellow about thirty years old, clutched a rifle. His legs were bowed so severely he rocked as he mounted the boulders.

The other man, an Aborigine who might have been in his sixties, moved steadily upward. He was wiry yet had the grace of a predator. The outback was filled with men like them, drifters who found the bush far removed from the law.

At the top, the elder found a cleft in the rock. From this cache he retrieved a board nearly as long as his arm. Ian had seen dancers perform with similar objects and knew they were supposed to be magical. The cubby surrendered perhaps a dozen other artifacts. All would fetch a small fortune on the black market.

While the older man worked steadily, the bowlegged bloke couldn't keep a proper watch. First he rubbed his nose with the back of his arm. Then he adjusted his shorts. He scanned the landscape, rifle at ready. Then he swatted a fly. Rubbed sweat through his hair. Tugged at his crotch. Abruptly he was alert again, scowling while the gun grew hot in the sun.

As they retreated, the Aborigine erased his footprints with a leafy branch. Ian let the SUV jangle out of sight before picking up the trail. They traveled faster now and corkscrewed across their original path. Where the spur intersected a paved road dusty tread marks headed toward the Stuart Highway, the only paved north-south road through the Territory. The pair could pick from dozens of unmarked byways. The artifacts would disappear.

Ian pushed the Land Rover to its limit. Although the old truck handled beautifully in the bush, it was as sluggish as a fly in winter. The needle was still climbing when Ian saw the red SUV parked beside the highway. If he pulled over, the men would surely notice when he followed them later.

The Toyota, a new model free of dents or scrapes, faced the road. The younger man smirked and the lines around his mouth twisted. Again Ian was struck by the elder's expression. White pipe clay severed his forehead and chin, and his face was a jigsaw of violence.

"So you've seen me," Ian murmured, "and I've seen you." He adjusted the rearview mirror but couldn't make out the tag number.

A roadhouse a quarter-hour away was a convenient place to watch for the men but they never appeared. It was possible they had turned east toward the coast. More likely they had dodged off into the bush. As night covered the sky, Ian had plenty of time to consider his next action.

He didn't need a fraction of it. The kangaroos could wait.

THOUSANDS OF KILOMETERS TO THE EAST, Gabriel Branch loaded the last of his bags into the hatchback. At six feet tall, Gabe barely fit behind the wheel even with the seat pushed all the way back. But the rear compartment was roomy enough to hold all his diving gear, and the hatch was easier to use than a station wagon. He squeezed in and steered for the coastal highway out of Townsville.

The next few days would be spent an hour or so south on the Whitsunday Islands. In the forty-five years Gabe had lived in Queensland, he rarely traveled more than a hundred kilometers inland. The neighbors never quite understood why his vacations didn't take advantage of the expansive desert at their back doors.

They didn't understand the...complications of Gabe's life. Oh, they knew about the Aboriginal land rights issues that had consumed the media for decades, and had heard about the children adopted by white families in a long-defunct effort to assimilate the race. But they didn't know what it was like to be caught by those issues against their will. Only a biracial Aborigine who had been assimilated at the age of three could tell them that. And Gabe wasn't talking.

Nor was he interested in drawing attention. Black faces were scarce in Australia, so he stuck close to the coastal cities that hosted international travelers in all their rainbow colors. He blended in better there and no one asked many questions about his background. Even when they did, they were met with silence.

Silence had kept his life on the smooth, orderly track he worked so hard to create. Last week he had hit a bump—a big bump—in his relationship with a Jamaican woman. Chance hadn't been in the country more than a few years. But she had some definite ideas about how much Gabe should say about his experiences and how loudly his voice should sound.

They had fought about it more of late. He supposed it was the same with all couples, as if money or household chores or work schedules were the cause of their problems instead of a symptom. Whatever the real reason, Gabe and Chance had split up last week. The separation was supposedly temporary, just a little breathing and thinking room, but Gabe knew where that would lead.

If Ian had been available, Gabe would have talked things over with him. In fifteen years of friendship, the men had seen each other through a number of breakups. None had been as serious as this one, though, and Gabe wished Ian would call. He already missed Chance's rapid-fire commentary and her odd machinegun laugh. Before the split, Gabe had been thinking of proposing. But courage in one person required courage in the other. And that, he knew, was the real reason their separation would be permanent.

When Ian did call, Gabe was already out of range. He heard only the clack of sugar cane as he sped past the coastal farms.

IAN TRACKED THE MEN FOR DAYS without coming within twenty kilometers of the truck. The outback was so big and its population so small, a little luck and a few calls let him keep tabs on the thieves as they passed through different roadhouses. At a tourist site called Devil's Marbles, a vendor remembered the odd pair and pointed to a faint track heading west.

When he located the Toyota, he parked some distance away and hiked in for a better look. Perhaps a dozen coffins had been removed from crevices in a wadi. The thieves were stealing bodies. Ian trotted back to the Land Rover and gunned the engine, all but honking to make sure they heard as he rattled toward the ridge.

The thieves took the hint. After the Toyota disappeared, Ian walked into the gully to inspect the damage. The coffins, each a cradle for the precious dead, were lined up in the center. Tarps and coils of rope had been left behind, along with cigarette butts and candy wrappers. The urine drying on the cliff face still smelled sharp.

Then Ian spotted the truck tucked under a ledge. It was the same one he had seen leave, he was sure of it. The guano he had noticed days earlier was still smeared on the side window. Yet the culvert had no other entrance except the one he had just walked through.

A bullet spun him off his feet. He heard nothing, not even the echo of the shot, as his shirt soaked in a red tide. The blood was brilliant at first, like the eyes of the metallic starlings that congregated around his boyhood home. He saw the Aborigine kneel beside him as his breath fled past his tongue.

The man was older than he had thought, much older, and carried with him the aura of ancient things. He wore only a string belt, a pair of shorts, and bands on his arms and legs. Tufts of cockatoo feathers framed a radiant face. On his chest a swirl of dots and circles, made hypnotic by his breath, pulled Ian into a galaxy of red.

He was terribly confused. He tried to separate the ringing in his head from his memories. *They ran away,* he thought. He had *seen* them drive across the plateau that drained west of the escarpment, had watched them until they were out of sight. The tire tracks he had crossed floated in his mind. Only one set of tracks, he realized. The truck had never left. How could he have been so wrong?

As if to offer comfort, the elder caressed Ian's forehead. The man's hair, shot with gray, looked nutmeg. It was as if his great age had worn the shine off the strands and leached away the pigment. His eyes were luminous, though, beyond the touch of time. Ian thought of the dingoes that gazed into his spotlight. The dogs always waited, knowing he would leave the kangaroo's heart and liver and kidneys for their feast.

Suddenly he understood. This man was a shaman. Ian had been lured into the culvert just as he had been tricked into speeding down the highway. He smiled and reached up.

"There, now," the man soothed, and flicked his blade across Ian's throat.

Other Works by Laine Cunningham

Nonfiction

Writing While Female or Black or Gay
Diverse Voices in Publishing
A twenty-year publishing professional's insights into the lack of diversity in publishing.

18,000 Miles
An Australia Travel Guide Companion to Woman Alone

Amazing Australia
A Traveler's Guide to Common Plants and Animals

On the Wallaby Track
An Essential Australian Slang Dictionary

Fiction

The Family Made of Dust
A Novel of Loss and Rebirth in the Australian Outback
When Gabriel Branch searches the outback for his best friend, he crosses paths with a tribal shaman who forces him to face the Aboriginal heritage he lost as a child.
Winner of two national awards.

Beloved
A Sensual Noir Thriller
A female FBI agent must access the dark power of the Hindu goddess Kali to bring a serial killer to justice.
Recipient of one arts grant.
Supported by two arts residencies.

Reparation

A Novel of Love, Devotion and Danger

A short vacation turns into a sinister game to save a sister and a lover from a peyote cult in this compulsive and compelling story about a Native American man.

Shortlisted for three national awards.

About the Author

For the past twenty years, Laine Cunningham has worked as a publishing consultant and ghostwriter through her company, Writer's Resource. At the same time, she built a career as a novelist. She has completed five book-length fiction projects so far, three of which are available in print and digital editions. Over the years her work has garnered eleven awards, been shortlisted sixteen times, and received dozens of residency programs and grants.

Laine's first novel*, The Family Made of Dust: A Novel of Loss and Rebirth in the Australian Outback,* is a work of literary suspense based on the Australian government's assimilation policy. Until early in the 1970s, biracial and light-skinned Aboriginal children were forcibly removed from their parents. In the novel, Gabriel Branch searches the outback for his best friend and stumbles on an artifact smuggling ring...and the Aboriginal heritage he lost as a child. *The Family Made of Dust* was called "the best novel in ten years" by the Hackney Literary Award committee. The James Jones Literary Society said it "demonstrates a mastery of psychological introspection and an uncanny feel for the spirit of place."

Readers interested in learning more about Aboriginal Dreamtime tales and how they can help modern societies might consider *Seven Sisters: Spiritual Messages from Aboriginal Australia.* In this collection, Laine pairs Dreamtime tales with essays that address universal issues like friendship, parenting, relationships and death.

Her second novel, *Beloved: A Sensual Noir Thriller,* follows an Indian- American FBI agent who sees visions from *The Ramayana,* a Hindu epic of good versus evil. Priya was led to law enforcement because she is the product of a gang-rape that occurred in India. While tracking a sadistic sexual predator, she accesses the dark powers of the goddess Kali. *Beloved* was supported by two residencies and one grant; it was shortlisted for three national awards.

Reparation: A Novel of Love, Devotion and Danger, is Laine's most recent work. Aidan Little Boy, a Lakota Sioux man, must stop the leader of a Native American-style peyote church before he enacts the largest mass murder ever to take place on US soil. *Reparation* was shortlisted for three national awards and has been compared to Terence Malick's *The New World.*

www.LaineCunningham.com

www.WritersResource.us

www.Patreon.com/LaineCunningham

Lightning Source UK Ltd.
Milton Keynes UK
UKOW05f1544211216
290553UK00014B/334/P

9 780998 224022